John Llewelyn Davies

The Epistles of St. Paul to the Ephesians, the Colossians, and Philemon

with introductions and notes, and an essay on the traces of foreign elements in the theology of these epistles

John Llewelyn Davies

The Epistles of St. Paul to the Ephesians, the Colossians, and Philemon
with introductions and notes, and an essay on the traces of foreign elements in the theology of these epistles

ISBN/EAN: 9783337381530

Printed in Europe, USA, Canada, Australia, Japan

Cover: Foto ©Lupo / pixelio.de

More available books at **www.hansebooks.com**

THE
EPISTLES OF ST. PAUL

TO

THE EPHESIANS, THE COLOSSIANS, AND PHILEMON:

WITH INTRODUCTIONS AND NOTES,

AND AN ESSAY ON THE TRACES OF FOREIGN ELEMENTS IN THE
THEOLOGY OF THESE EPISTLES.

BY THE

REV. J. LLEWELYN DAVIES, M.A.

RECTOR OF CHRIST CHURCH, ST. MARYLEBONE;
LATE FELLOW OF TRINITY COLLEGE, CAMBRIDGE.

London:
MACMILLAN AND CO.
1866.

LONDON
R. CLAY, SON, AND TAYLOR, PRINTERS,
BREAD STREET HILL.

PREFACE.

THE chief object which I have had in view in preparing this volume has been to draw attention to the subject-matter of the Epistles to the Ephesians and Colossians. The theology of St. Paul is here stated with a largeness which adapts it, I conceive, in a special manner to the inquiries of the present time. Whether Creation has any centre and ground; whether human life has any key and pattern,—are questions which belong peculiarly to the speculations of this age, and to which these Epistles offer a common answer by setting forth CHRIST in universal relations of a twofold kind,—as the Word who is the law and life of the universal creation, and as the Son who is the head of universal humanity. This edition seeks to further in some humble measure the study of that answer. I have doubted myself, and therefore I cannot be surprised if others should doubt, whether what I have been able to contribute towards this object is sufficient to justify the publication of an independent edition of these Epistles. But I hope there may be some students to whom an edition offering the kind of illustration which I have attempted to supply, and omitting what I have left to works of higher pretensions, may not be unacceptable. I have endeavoured to avoid the appearance of entering into rivalry with editions in which the true text of the Epistles is discussed, the opinions of previous interpreters recorded, and questions arising out of the text investigated. At the same time I have done my best to explain the letter of the Epistles, not treating them technically, but endeavouring to regard them simply as documents of the highest value which it is by no means easy to understand. When we are desirous of obtaining a conception of a document as a whole, there is a certain advantage in putting aside discussions which, however valuable for their special purposes, may have the effect of expanding details into inconvenient magnitude.

I have printed the text of Tischendorf, as having on the whole the best claim at the present moment to the character of a received text.

The translations have been made with an eye to the object of this edition, and are intended simply to aid the modern reader in arriving at the substantial sense of the writer. They therefore do not challenge close verbal criticism as revised translations.

CONTENTS.

	PAGE
GENERAL INTRODUCTION	1
INTRODUCTION TO THE EPISTLE TO THE EPHESIANS	9
THE TEXT, WITH NOTES	27
TRANSLATION	65
INTRODUCTION TO THE EPISTLE TO THE COLOSSIANS	77
THE TEXT, WITH NOTES	87
TRANSLATION	113
INTRODUCTION TO THE EPISTLE TO PHILEMON	121
THE TEXT, WITH NOTES	123
TRANSLATION	127
ON THE TRACES OF FOREIGN ELEMENTS IN THE DOCTRINE OF THESE EPISTLES; AND ESPECIALLY ON THE GNOSTICAL TERMS OCCURRING IN THEM	129

GENERAL INTRODUCTION.

FOUR of St. Paul's extant letters—those to the Ephesians, the Colossians, Philemon, and the Philippians — were written, according to the general belief, at nearly the same time of his life, and when he was in nearly the same circumstances. Three of them were to be carried by the same hands. Tychicus is the messenger sent to the Church at Ephesus (Eph. vi. 21, 22); Tychicus and Onesimus are sent to Colossæ (Col. iv. 7—9); Onesimus is sent with the letter to his master Philemon. These three profess to be written by a prisoner (Eph. vi. 20; Col. iv. 18; Philemon, 1); and the imprisonment is shared by Aristarchus (Col. iv. 10). We learn from Acts xxvii. 2, that Aristarchus had accompanied St. Paul on his voyage to Rome. The imprisonment, therefore, to which reference is made in these letters is apparently that which continued for two years at Rome. The letter to the Church at Philippi was also written by one who was in bonds, and contains allusions to the imperial court and household (Phil. i. 13, iv. 22), which prove that it was written during the same imprisonment.

This imprisonment is thus described in the concluding words of the Acts:—"And Paul dwelt two whole years (διετίαν ὅλην) in his own hired house, and received all that came in unto him, preaching the kingdom of God and teaching those things which concern the Lord Jesus Christ with all confidence, no man forbidding him." It is certainly the natural inference from this statement that the imprisonment terminated in some way at the end of the two years.

If the writer had meant only that the imprisonment had continued for two years up to the time of his writing the conclusion of his history, he would in all probability have expressed himself differently. He would not have rounded the period of time by calling it διετία ὅλη. We have therefore a space of two years within which to place the writing of these four letters. The date of St. Paul's arrival at Rome can be fixed with great certainty. It is proved, by Wieseler* and others, that Felix was recalled from Judæa and succeeded by Festus in A.D. 60. St. Paul left Cæsarea in the autumn of that year. In the spring therefore of A.D. 61 he arrived at Rome, and his sojourn there must have lasted till the spring of A.D. 63. There are reasons for believing that the Epistle to the Philippians was written towards the end of this period. We have no materials for fixing more precisely the common date of the other three.

The condition of St. Paul as a prisoner at Rome was in one point extremely galling, but in other respects he was treated with special indulgence and consideration. In accordance with the Roman method of guarding prisoners, he was bound by a chain to a soldier, from whom it would seem that he could never be separated by night or by day. The chain was fastened to the right wrist of the prisoner and to the left wrist of the soldier. When St. Paul was first taken into custody at Jerusalem, he was bound with two such chains, one to each hand (Acts xxi. 33). The hand which he stretched forth when he spoke before Agrippa was loaded with a chain—"except these bonds" (Acts xxvi. 29). At Rome, "Paul was suffered to dwell by himself with the soldier that kept him" (Acts xxviii. 16). In the Epistle to the Ephesians he says that he discharged his office of ambassador in behalf of the gospel "in a chain" (ἐν

---

* Chronologie des Apostolischen Zeitalters, pp. 66 and foll.

ἁλύσει). If, as seems probable, St. Paul was never released for an hour during those two years from so oppressive an incubus, he might well insist upon his bonds as a kind of martyrdom in the cause of Christ, which entitled him to the more affectionate deference on the part of his fellow-believers. But the inevitable annoyance of such custody was mitigated by a greater degree of liberty than would have been compatible, without such an expedient, with any confinement at all. From the first, the evident nobleness of the Apostle's character had won him considerate and courteous treatment at the hands of the Roman officials. At Cæsarea he had liberty to see his friends without restriction (Acts xxiv. 23). On the voyage to Rome Julius, the centurion in command, began by using him kindly (φιλανθρώπως χρησάμενος—Acts xxvii. 3), and must have ended by regarding him with profound respect and gratitude. After he had arrived at Rome, he was almost as free for his work of preaching Christ and directing the Churches as if he had been his own master.

During the two years of this imprisonment at Rome, then, we are to think of St. Paul as never enjoying complete privacy, but as continually occupied at his will in proclaiming the kingdom of God to all who would come to him, in expounding the doctrine of Christ to Jews and Gentiles, in receiving envoys from Churches in Greece and in Asia, in sending messages and writing letters to all who needed his counsel.* This was by no means an inactive or

---

* It has been asked why the group of kindred Epistles to the Ephesians, the Colossians, and Philemon, might not have been written whilst St. Paul was kept bound at Cæsarea, before he was conveyed to Rome. During that earlier part of his imprisonment, he was not prevented from communicating with his friends, and we cannot say that Aristarchus was *not* with him at Cæsarea, as well as at Rome. But we gather from these Epistles that whilst he was writing them St. Paul was labouring freely and actively in his apostolic work, and that others were co-operating with him in that work (Eph. vi. 19, 20 ; Col. iv. 11). Now we have seen that the conclusion of the Acts describes him as enjoying this freedom at Rome, and the Epistle to the Philippians, which is evidently written

unfruitful portion of his apostolic life. The Apostle of the Gentiles had long wished earnestly to visit Rome, the metropolis of the Gentile world; probably his "appeal to Cæsar" was dictated in part by this desire. He came as a prisoner, but it was so ordered that his bonds, instead of hindering the work for which he lived, turned out "rather unto the furtherance of the gospel" (Phil. i. 12). A very few out of the many letters which it is reasonable to suppose that he wrote, have been preserved for the permanent instruction of the Church; these, like the rest, the writer would have us remember, were written with his right hand "in a chain."

We find little necessity in the writings of St. Paul for dwelling on contemporary secular history. His letters do not happen to contain allusions to historical persons or events. But it is certain that he was not indifferent to what was going on in the world around him. Whilst he was at Rome, Nero was the Cæsar for whose judgment he was waiting; and Nero at that time was advancing rapidly from bad to worse. In A.D. 59 he had put his mother Agrippina to death. He then plunged into unseemly riot, degrading his rank by appearing as a musical performer on the stage, and corrupting all about him with shameful and brutal excesses. In the year 62, Burrus, the commander of that *prætorium* to which St. Paul alludes (Phil. i. 13), died ("incertum valetudine an veneno,"—Tacitus, Annals, xiv. 51); and one of the few honest men in high place was succeeded by one of the most infamous, Tigellinus being raised to the vacant command. In the same year

---

from Rome, speaks of the great success which had attended his efforts and those of his fellow-labourers (Phil. i. 12—14). On the other hand, there is no mention of his having been allowed so large a liberty at Cæsarea. The verse in the Acts only says (ἢ προσέρχεσθαι being omitted in the truer text) that the centurion was to keep him and show him indulgence, and forbid none of his connexions to do him services. The scenery of these Epistles therefore agrees much better with the imprisonment at Rome than with that at Cæsarea.

Seneca sought and obtained permission to retire from the court. It was the misfortune of Seneca to live in a fearfully corrupt age and to have a Nero for his pupil. His admirable ethical philosophy is tacked on like a *purpureus pannus* to the life of Nero, as if to exhibit the weakness and failure of the very best Pagan sentiment in that age, and to serve as a contrast to the message which, though foolishness to the Greeks, proved itself to be the power of God. Seneca was in all probability the brother of the Gallio who protected St. Paul in Achaia; and he may have heard of the Apostle himself. If he did, it is scarcely possible that the courtier-philosopher could have regarded the Jewish prisoner with other feelings than those of serene indifference. His writings, however, have so much that resembles the language of Christian morality as to have given rise to the report that he was acquainted with St. Paul. This supposition has found a record in some spurious letters of Seneca to Paul. When Seneca withdrew into retirement, Nero probably felt one more restraint taken off. He proceeded immediately to divorce and put to death his innocent wife Octavia. The great conflagration at Rome, attributed to Nero himself, and famous in Christian annals because the blame of it was laid by Nero upon the Christians, took place in the year which followed the termination of St. Paul's imprisonment. The revelations of Tacitus and Juvenal, though they do not illustrate details (except indeed the names of vices) in the writings of St. Paul, are most important as enabling us to realize in the midst of what kind of surrounding element he taught and wrote and did his apostolic work.

The history in the Acts tells us that even at Rome his own countrymen were St. Paul's first care, and that he followed there his old plan of giving them the first offer of his Gospel. There was a great multitude of Jews at Rome, and the Apostle invited the chief of them to come and hear him. The answer made by the Jews is one of the principal difficulties in the Acts, professing as it does a degree of ignorance on their part both of St. Paul himself and of the faith of the Christians, which seems hardly consistent with the status of the Church at Rome as we learn it from the Epistle to the Romans. No doubt can reasonably be thrown upon the existence of a recognised Church at Rome. But it may have been comparatively insignificant in so vast a place. It may have consisted almost entirely of persons who had received the Gospel first elsewhere; and there may have been no attempt, previous to St. Paul's arrival, to proclaim Jesus as the Christ amongst the Jews settled at Rome. These suppositions may in part explain the answer of the Jews, "We neither received letters out of Judæa concerning thee, neither any of the brethren that came shewed or spake any harm of thee. But we desire to hear of thee what thou thinkest: for as concerning this sect, we know that everywhere it is spoken against." There will still linger perhaps in our minds some surprise that the name of Paul should not have been better known amongst the chief of his countrymen at Rome. But he unquestionably had many friends there, already worshipping the same Saviour with himself; some of whom had come to meet him "as far as Appii Forum and the Three Taverns," causing Paul to "thank God and take courage."

We observe that the historian of the Acts describes *the teaching* of St. Paul at Rome in the oldest and simplest terms of the Christian creed. To proclaim the kingdom of God, and to tell men concerning the Lord Jesus Christ, this was still the main work of St. Paul (Acts xxviii. 23, 31). But it is an interesting question, whether he was now contemplating the kingdom of God and the Lord Jesus Christ in exactly the same way as he had done in Greece or Asia Minor or Palestine. For the answering of this question our only materials are the four letters written during this imprisonment. The Epistle to Philemon, though most valuable on other grounds, has no special theological significance. The Epistle to the Philippians is rich in practical theology, and has its own marked features. If we compare this with those to the Ephesians and Colossians, we may find many resemblances between them. But these would be chiefly in points which all the letters of St. Paul have in common. Indeed, the general theological aspect of the Epistle to the Philippians is at least as similar to that of the Epistles to the Corinthians as to that of its more contemporaneous Epistles. But when we compare together the Epistles to the Ephesians and the Colossians, we not only perceive them to be strikingly alike externally and in details, but they seem to have in common a certain type of doctrine distinguishable from that of the other writings of St. Paul. It is difficult indeed to say, considering the patent coincidences of expression in the two Epistles, whether the points of likeness or of unlikeness between them are the more remarkable. No one can doubt that either one Epistle was an intentional copy of the other, or else both were written at very nearly the same time by the same author. It is when we are considering the doctrinal substance of the Epistles that the latter conclusion forces itself upon us most irresistibly as the true one. These two letters are twins, singularly like one another in face, like also in character, but not so identical as to exclude a strongly marked individuality.

The scheme of construction is the same in the two Epistles. Each of them is divisible into two parts, of which the former declares how God has revealed himself—especially in relation to men—in Christ; the latter appeals to us to live in conformity with what has been thus manifested. The author, in preparing to write, has set distinctly before his mind the image of CHRIST, the Son of God, the Head of men. Whatever can be read in the person of Christ, *that* he affirms without reserve both concerning the

Father and concerning men. All the qualities and acts and experiences of Christ assume an infinite importance when interpreted in this twofold relation. St. Paul contemplates in Christ the full mind of the Father; he sees in his filial nature *our* sonship to God, in his death *our* death to the old natural state, in his resurrection *our* rising again to a new life, in his ascension *our* exaltation to a heavenly sphere of existence, in his reign the pledge of a perfect triumph of order over disorder, of good over evil. The Son, making God the Father known to men; the Son, explaining men to themselves, and restoring them to a right relation towards God and one another,—is the centre of thought in these Epistles. Nothing can be more orderly, nothing, in the higher sense, more systematic, than the reference of everything in heaven and earth, of all divinity and all morality, of the perfect ideal of God and the lamentable aberrations of men, to the one nature and life of Christ,—which we may trace throughout these writings. St. Paul had always, from the time of his conversion, worshipped the Lord Jesus Christ as the Son of God and the Lord of men; but at the time when he wrote these letters, the conception of Christ as gathering up in himself all that has ever come forth from the creative mind of the one God and Father seems to have been most distinct to his thoughts, and to have filled the whole capacity of his intellect most completely. There is such a vastness, however, in this conception, that it is susceptible of very various applications; and the clear differences between the profound and magnificent ideas of the one and the other of these Epistles make it almost impossible for an earnest student to look upon either as a copyist's imitation of the other.

INTRODUCTION TO THE EPISTLE TO THE EPHESIANS.

This Epistle professes to be written by St. Paul. It not only begins with a salutation given in his name, but it contains a long and remarkable passage (iii. 1—13) in which he describes the commission he had received as the Apostle of the Gentiles, and appeals to the sufferings of his imprisonment as adding weight to his exhortations and reflecting dignity upon the common cause. No other Epistle bears a more distinct profession of being St. Paul's than this does. It has been maintained, nevertheless, by distinguished critics (including De Wette and Ewald) that this is not a genuine work of St. Paul.

Those who cannot read the Epistle to the Ephesians without being awed by the peculiar loftiness, by the grandeur of conception, by the profound insight, by the eucharistic inspiration, which they recognise in it, will require strong evidence to persuade them that it was written by some other man who wished it to pass as St. Paul's. Apart from the question of the morality of the act, imitators do not pour out their thoughts in the free and fervid style of this Epistle. Nor can we easily imagine how such an imitation could have been successful either near the time of St. Paul, or at any subsequent period. It is not conceivable that it should have made its appearance without exciting wonder and inquiry. In the lifetime of St. Paul the pious fraud would not have been attempted. Within a few years after his death, the difficulty of deceiving his friends and the

Church in such a matter must have been very great. At a later time, the estimation in which St. Paul's writings were held would have ensured the careful scrutiny of any previously unknown work put forward in his name. And there are no signs that the genuineness of the Epistle to the Ephesians was ever doubted in the Church. The external testimonies to it are neither inadequate nor obscure. Not to lay stress on the apparent allusions in Polycarp and Ignatius, there are formal quotations from this Epistle, as St. Paul's to the Ephesians, in Irenæus [*] and Clement of Alexandria,[†] which prove that in their time, that is, in the latter part of the second century, this work was universally received as genuine. Some recent critics are the only persons who have ever suspected it to be spurious. These considerations then,—the profession of being St. Paul's wrought into the texture of the Epistle, its wonderfully genuine air, the difficulty of imposing a spurious Epistle of St. Paul upon the Church, the positive external testimony of ancient writers, and the absence of any doubt in the Church,—are in favour of the genuineness of this Epistle.

The arguments on the other side may be reduced to three. (1) We miss the characteristics which we should expect in any letter of St. Paul's, and especially in a letter to the Christians of Ephesus. (2) There are differences between the thoughts and the style of this work and those of St. Paul's other writings. (3) There is a suspicious resemblance between this and the Epistle to the Colossians.

(1) It is certainly very strange that in writing to the Ephesians St. Paul should have omitted all references to

[*] Τοῦτο δὲ καὶ ὁ Παῦλος λέγει· πᾶν γὰρ τὸ φανερούμενον φῶς ἐστίν (Eph. v. 13). Irenæus adv. Hær. i. 8. 5. Καθὼς ὁ μακάριος Παῦλός φησιν, ἐν τῇ πρὸς Ἐφεσίους ἐπιστολῇ· ὅτι μέλη ἐσμὲν τοῦ σώματος, ἐκ τῆς σαρκὸς αὐτοῦ, καὶ ἐκ τῶν ὀστέων αὐτοῦ (Eph. v. 30.) Ibid. v. 2, 3.

[†] After quoting a passage from the 2d Epistle to the Corinthians, Clement adds, σαφέστατα δὲ Ἐφεσίοις γράφων ἀπεκάλυψε τὸ ζητούμενον ὧδέ πως λέγων· μέχρι καταντήσωμεν οἱ πάντες κ.τ.λ. (Eph. iv. 13—15), Pæd. i. 18. See also Strom. iv. 65.

particular members of the Church at Ephesus, and to particular circumstances affecting it. If there was one Church with which St. Paul was personally intimate, we might say it was the Church at Ephesus. Labours, dangers, and successes had united their threefold influence in endearing to him the body of believers in that city. We should read two chapters in the Acts, the 19th and 20th, to revive the recollection of the character of St. Paul's connexion with Ephesus. It was quite impossible for him, whose memory of all fellowship in trial and affection was so strong and enduring, to forget those for whom he had suffered and striven so much, and who had loved him in return so heartily. In writing to the Corinthians, when he wants an example of the worst things he has endured, he refers to his "fight with wild beasts" at Ephesus. In that most touching address which he made to the Ephesian elders at Miletus, he says himself, "Remember that by the space of three years I ceased not to warn every one night and day with tears." And his parting from them is thus described, "When he had thus spoken, he kneeled down, and prayed with them all. And they all wept sore, and fell on Paul's neck, and kissed him, sorrowing most of all for the words which he spake, that they should see his face no more. And they accompanied him to the ship." Can it be, we ask, that in writing to the Christians of a place where there had been so much to stir his speculative intellect, his moral energies, his affectionate sympathy, so much to raise his office and his endowments in his own eyes, he should show a forgetfulness which is so singularly unlike him, and should never once refer to any particular person or to any local circumstance?

The closest scrutiny of the Epistle has discovered little to modify the impression of strangeness thus made upon us. It is true that the history in the Acts exhibits a prevalence at Ephesus of magical delusions, an activity of superstition, which some of the special doctrine in the Epistle to the Ephesians is well calculated to meet. The thought of evil spiritual powers working in the invisible world (Eph. ii. 2, vi. 12) might be suggested by the exorcising of evil spirits and the use of magical formulas of which we read in the Acts (xix. 13, 19). Some coincidences also may be found between the language of the address to the elders at Miletus and that of the Epistle. But these correspondences are slight in themselves, and do not at all fill up the place of the personal allusions which might have been expected and are wanting.

One important hint which the text of the Epistle supplies for a solution of this difficulty, is to be found in the absence from some MSS. of the words ἐν Ἐφέσῳ in the salutation. If these are removed, there remains no evidence that this Epistle was written to the Ephesians at all. It still professes to be written by St. Paul; but, for anything we know, it might have been addressed to Christians who had never seen him. Now St. Basil* says that there was a tradition that these two words should be omitted, and that he had so read the passage in ancient MSS. There are more doubtful intimations to the same effect in Jerome and Tertullian. In accordance with this evidence, these words are omitted in the original writing in two of the most important MSS.—the Vatican and the Sinaitic. An attempt was made, as we find in St. Basil and St. Jerome, to read the passage as if it were complete without ἐν Ἐφέσῳ or any substitute for these words, by laying an emphasis on τοῖς οὖσιν. But no one will suppose that the author intended this. The question suggested by the partial omission of ἐν Ἐφέσῳ has been whether the Epistle might not have been written for other communities besides the Church at Ephesus. If it was to be sent even to one other church, as that of Laodicea; and still more, if it was to be read to several of

* Cont. Eunom. ii. 19.

the churches in the neighbourhood of Ephesus, both the absence of special allusions and the MS. uncertainty about ἐν Ἐφέσῳ would be sufficiently accounted for.

The expression in iii. 3, 4, "As I wrote before in few words, whereby when ye read ye may understand my knowledge in the mystery of Christ," is generally taken to refer to what St. Paul had just written, chiefly in the first chapter; and no doubt this is quite possible. But the first impression of the ordinary reader would be, I think, that St. Paul was referring to some other document. Is it allowable to conjecture that St. Paul had quite recently written a more special letter to the Ephesians, and that he had said in that whatever of a special nature he wished to communicate to them? It is true that in that case we cannot say why he should have sent another epistle to them; but supposing him to have been led by any unknown circumstance to do so, it was needless to repeat what he had said before, and he was at liberty to pour out a more unbroken stream of doctrine.

(2) A second argument against the genuineness of this Epistle is founded upon the differences between the thoughts and the language of this and those of St. Paul's acknowledged writings. It is assumed in this argument that the Epistle to the Colossians is not taken into account. The Epistle to the Ephesians, it is urged, is *too like* this, *too unlike* the rest.

The differences which are appealed to are real, and such as no one need wish to deny; but conclusions drawn from the critical observation of likenesses and unlikenesses are extremely unstable. Lists of words not used elsewhere by the same writer are almost contemptible as evidence of spuriousness. If these ἅπαξ λεγόμενα were used obtrusively, they might be an indication of a writer so attached to particular words that he could write nothing without bringing them in; but if they fitly express the thoughts of the writer, is he to be debarred from entertaining the new idea, or from using the terms appropriate to it? The *feeling* of a critic who is thoroughly familiar with the writings in question is of far more weight. But we have had abundant cautions not to defer too easily in such matters to personal authority. The conclusion of the critic depends not only upon his learning, taste, and honesty, but also upon his antecedent bias and upon assumptions which may be very questionable.

When we survey the whole body of the letters professing to be written by St. Paul, we cannot but be struck by the varieties of style to be observed amongst them; and the impression is deepened when we consider within how short a time they are all supposed to have been written. St. Paul was past middle life,—he may have been fifty years of age,—when the first of his Epistles was written; he had then been a Christian for not less than fourteen years; and all the Epistles were written within a space of perhaps seventeen years. That in a collection of writings composed under these conditions there should be such varieties of thought and style as there are in the Pauline Epistles, is a phenomenon to which we could hardly find a parallel in literature.* But these writings differ amongst themselves in such a way as to make it very difficult to draw a line which shall place all the letters which have a clear stamp of common authorship on one side, and the rest on the other. For example, if we suppose the Epistle to the Ephesians to be rejected on the evidence of its style and ideas, what is to be done with that to the Colossians? It would be no easy matter to decide which of these two Epistles is the more unlike those to the Romans and Corinthians. If we advance with modern criticism to its farthest point, and

---

* M. Renan, who only rejects the Pastoral Epistles, speaks of St. Paul's Epistles as written within a space of eleven years, between A.D. 53 and A.D. 62. *Les Apôtres*, p. v.

pronounce all the Epistles to be spurious except the four to the Romans, Corinthians, and Galatians, we may find it difficult to maintain that the Epistle to the Philippians is manifestly further removed than that to the Galatians in tone and style from the Second to the Corinthians. And however decided the differences we may be able to perceive between the four groups of Pauline Letters (1 and 2 Thessalonians, —Romans, 1 and 2 Corinthians, Galatians,—Ephesians, Colossians, Philemon, Philippians,—1 and 2 Timothy, Titus), we can hardly fail to recognise their mutual likeness when we compare them with any other writings, whether with the other Epistles of the New Testament Canon, or with any compositions outside of the Canon. If we took any two of the Pauline Epistles, as Romans and 2 Timothy, and compared them together, we should have less difficulty in ascribing them both to the same author, than in ascribing either of them to any other author whom we know.

Let us suppose that the reader feels the alleged diversities to be real and surprising, and yet that the evidence for the Pauline authorship of all these letters appears to him almost irresistible,—may he not reasonably reckon this variety as one amongst the wonderful phenomena which the history of St. Paul presents? There are many things in the character and life of St. Paul which would be incredible, if we had not good evidence that they are true: and the *versatility* of his mind, its quick and pliant response to every new demand made upon his attention or his sympathy, has always seemed one of the most wonderful of his qualities. The undoubted tenacity and constancy of his nature makes this versatility the more remarkable. We ought to expect, therefore, that he would write very differently under different circumstances. Let us take into consideration also what the due effect of his *inspiration* would be. Such an influence would naturally make a man less of a machine, less uniform and same in his thoughts and utterances. Under each new impression, in each new situation, he would be more thoroughly possessed and moulded by his conviction than an uninspired man. There would be stronger marks of personality, and yet the man would be so moved by the conditions surrounding him that he might appear to be one person at one time and another person at another time. These considerations may help us to admit to the full the diversities which critics have observed in the Pauline Epistles, and yet not to draw the inference that any of them are spurious.

(3) We need to bear the same reflections in mind whilst we consider the third argument brought against the genuineness of the Epistle to the Ephesians,—its suspicious relation to the Epistle to the Colossians. The resemblances between the two Epistles do not need to be pointed out; they are obvious on the surface. The two compositions are constructed upon the same lines, and to a great extent the same material is worked up in them. But these resemblances seem to agree far less with the hypothesis that one is a copy of the other than with that of their being written at very nearly the same time by the same person. Nothing is more frequent than for letters written at the same time to different correspondents to have a great deal both of thought and language in common. The leading ideas in each Epistle are sufficiently distinguishable from one another, and in each the thoughts and phrases which are common to both are in perfect harmony with the subject. It is more difficult to account for the difference in style, which appears to be considerable. (See the Introduction to Colossians.) St. Paul, we shall be obliged to say, was a man who would write on one day as he does to the Colossians, and on the next day as he does to the Ephesians.

As to the relative priority of the two Epistles, the

presumptions on either side are scarcely strong enough to warrant a confident conclusion. That a very short interval separated them will be doubted by no one who believes that St. Paul wrote both, and we may be content to leave it undecided which was written first.

It is to be remembered that in writing to Ephesus St. Paul was in effect writing to the province of which Ephesus was the leading city. Its importance in this character was manifestly the reason why St. Paul spent so long a time teaching there. We read in the account of his stay at Ephesus (Acts xix. 10), "This continued by the space of two years; so that *all they which dwelt in Asia* heard the word of the Lord Jesus, both Jews and Greeks." And the same circumstance is mentioned in the speech of Demetrius, "Ye see and hear, that not alone at Ephesus, but *almost throughout all Asia*, this Paul hath persuaded and turned away much people" (Ibid. ver. 26). It may be supposed therefore that St. Paul, when remembering the Ephesian Church, was led to consider the state of mind prevailing throughout that part of Asia Minor, and the dangers which beset the believers dwelling in that country. An ancient Asiatic goddess, called Artemis by the Greeks and Diana by the Romans, but whose clumsy image, shaped like a mummy, and adorned with many breasts and the figures of various animals, symbolized the productive and nutritive powers of Nature, was highly honoured at Ephesus, and also "throughout all Asia." But neither in this Epistle, nor in the two to Timothy, is there any unmistakeable allusion to the worship of this local divinity. The believers whom St. Paul was addressing had either never paid homage to the Ephesian idol, or were emancipated from its fascination. Perhaps, however, the superstition to which they had been accustomed might make them more ready to accept such schemes of opposed hierarchies of good and evil spirits as were attracting the Jewish mind in that age. So far as we can gather from the Epistles to Timothy, written to him as presiding over the Church at Ephesus, and from this Epistle, the dangerous speculations which occurred to the writer's mind were those of Orientalized Judaism. "I besought thee," says St. Paul, "to abide at Ephesus, that thou mightest charge some not to give heed to fables and endless genealogies, ($\mu\acute{u}\theta οις καὶ γενεαλογίαις ἀπεράντοις,$) which minister questions" (1 Tim. i. 3, 4). Compare "*Jewish* fables" in Titus i. 14. Again in 1 Tim. vi. 4 and 20, we have allusions to a morbid love of "questions and strifes of words" ($ζητήσεις καὶ λογομαχίας$, see also 2 Tim. ii. 23), and to "the profane babblings and oppositions of the falsely-named knowledge or Gnosis," ($ἀντιθέσεις τῆς ψευδωνύμου γνώσεως.$) Speculative theories about emanations, one series being *opposed* to another, having their ultimate origin in Oriental, probably Persic, theosophy, but coming through Jewish channels, would best answer to these descriptions.

The Apocalypse, the Epistles of St. John, and the Gospel of St. John, are all associated with Ephesus, but they do not happen to supply any special illustrations to the Epistle to the Ephesians. The Apocalypse was probably written a very few years after this Epistle. Ephesus stands first in the list of the Seven Churches in Asia to which special messages are given. But the message to the angel of the Church of Ephesus contains nothing to remind us of St. Paul's Epistle. In the Laodicean message, the titles assumed by the Son of Man, "the Amen, the faithful and true Witness, the beginning ($ἀρχή$) of the Creation of God," resemble the doctrine of this Epistle, but are more directly parallel to the language of the Epistle to the Colossians. The Epistles and the Gospel of St. John were written at a much later period. It is most interesting to compare their theology with that of the letters of St. Paul which we are now considering, but the aged St. John is dealing with the speculations of a later date in the history of the Church, and his teaching is intended to convey developments of the truth, and to correct errors, which had more than a local character.

It is implied in what has been already said, that we find no clear intimation in this Epistle of any special questions to be settled, or of any peculiar faults or dangers against which the writer desired to warn his readers. It is remarkable as a free spontaneous utterance of Christian thought, exercised upon the great topics of God's purposes and man's duty. It is possible that his subject, or rather his manner of treating it, may have been partly suggested to the Apostle by the modes of thought prevalent in the Church of Asia Minor. Perhaps what he knew of the mind of that Church gave him at least greater freedom in pouring forth, as into sympathising ears, the thoughts of which his own heart was full. But there are very slight grounds for connecting the substance of this Epistle with any decided peculiarity of the Ephesian Christians. And in reading it we are scarcely led to look for any other motive than the fervour of a devout spirit delighting to give expression to the impulses of faith and love. Indeed it would be hardly extravagant to regard this work as a Hymn. Though the form of the composition is that of a letter, the mood of the writer is lyrical rather than hortatory. From time to time the eucharistic strain which pervades the whole Epistle rises into rhythmic solemnity; and the diction is throughout somewhat more poetical than in the other writings of St. Paul.

The key to the Epistle may be found in the opening sentence. After the salutation, St. Paul begins his psalm with the words, "Blessed be God and the Father of our Lord Jesus Christ, who has blessed us with all spiritual blessing in heavenly things in Christ." Fixing his eyes on the Lord Jesus Christ, he opens his mind to the blessings which radiate forth from him, and from the Father through him, upon the whole world. The mind of God towards men unveiled in Christ, the relation of men towards God exhibited in Christ, the present spiritual connexion of men with Christ, the hopes of which Christ is the ground and assurance, the laws imposed by the life of Christ upon human life,—these are the blessings for which he gives thanks. Christ embracing humanity in himself is the subject of the Epistle. The difficulties which it presents to the reader reside in the mystery of these relations of Christ to mankind. The Sonship of Christ to the Father is assumed but not dwelt upon; we have here to do with what may be read in the Person of Christ concerning the nature and destiny of man, when Christ is received as the eternal Son of God.

St. Paul tells us with strict faithfulness what he has thus *read* in Christ. He draws his inferences rationally from what he believes he has seen. There is not the slightest appearance of anything *composite* in his system of doctrine. Christ, with the effects which radiate from him, fills the whole sphere of his mind. The relations of which he speaks are indeed, as he continually reminds us, spiritual, heavenly, or mystical. But they form in his conception a living organic unity. If we recognise this, although it may be profoundly interesting to observe points of connexion in ideas or phrases with the speculations of Philo or the Gnostics, it is impossible to father the doctrine of St. Paul upon Alexandrian or Persian theosophy. As it is also inconceivable that any writer should have either felt or feigned such a joyful and absorbing thankfulness as St. Paul expresses for what had been revealed to him through Christ, if he had borrowed this notion and that from the philosophies current in his age. If ever any theory of human nature was *original*, St. Paul's in this Epistle has a right to be called so.

A summary statement of this doctrine, however bald and inadequate, may serve the useful purpose of keeping the main features of it before the mind. It may be presented in the following form :—

God sent his Son into the world in our flesh and blood. Jesus Christ, the Son of God, lived, died, rose from the dead, was exalted to the right hand of the Father, and then came again, in the outpouring of the promised Spirit, and accompanying the word of his heralds.

1. We infer from these facts a fatherly mind in God towards human nature, and therefore that men *are* God's children.

2. We infer that God intended men to be spiritually on the footing of sons towards himself, knowing him and loving him.

3. Men have evidently been estranged from God, but by sending his Son into the world and giving him up to die, God has shewn a purpose to bring them out of estrangement into the true filial state.

4. In raising Christ from the dead, and lifting him above the visible world, God has set Christ supreme above death and the world. *The will and power which thus wrought, must, in virtue of God's eternal purpose and the connexion between Christ and the human race, go on to confer a new life and a heavenly exaltation on men, Christ's brethren and members.*

5. This raising and exalting of men is already, in the creative idea of God, done in Christ. It is realized in successive generations through men's conscious acceptance of this grace, or through faith.

6. The true conception of mankind is that of a family bound by invisible links of creation to Christ and sharing his life, and therefore calling God Father. The duty of men is to act in harmony with these relations.

7. The Will of God manifested in Christ, though it has

signally triumphed and must prevail, is now contending against rebellious wills. Every man who is called to the knowledge of God is also enlisted in a warfare against evil.

These propositions, I believe, express the leading ideas of St. Paul's teaching in this Epistle. Lest the reader should be disposed to pass by what might be called the mystical element in the propositions numbered (4) and (5), it is important to observe that this idea,—whatever difficulty we may find in apprehending it, and however fanciful it may seem to a modern philosopher,—is absolutely central to St. Paul's system. An Eternal Will, entering creatively into time, unfolding itself through opposition, holding fast its aim; this Will adequately manifested in Christ; Christ the Divine Man, whose perfectly loyal nature is the key to the mysteries of men's disordered nature;—St. Paul held these to be the invisible realities out of which all visible phenomena had their growth, and from which the history of the future was to be inferred.

The chief natural division of the Epistle, and one which was probably designed by the writer, is at the end of the 3d chapter. In the former half St. Paul describes the vocation or calling of Christians, in the latter he appeals to his readers to walk worthily of it. Some such division is very common in St. Paul's writings. It is his invariable principle to lay down first the relations which God has established, and then to deduce from these the conduct appropriate to them. But the division is more strict in this Epistle than in any other. The latter half may be further subdivided for convenience, and each repetition of the injunction, "Walk therefore," (iv. 1; iv. 17; v. 1, 2; v. 15,) may be taken as commencing a fresh appeal, down to the concluding paragraph (vi. 10). The subdivisions of the former half are more important to notice. The distinct paragraphs end as follows: at i. 14, at i. 23, at ii. 10, at

ii. 22, and at iii. 21 : the division at the end of the first chapter being less strongly marked than the others.

In the first paragraph, St. Paul sets forth in comprehensive words the blessings, in the past, the present, and the future, which belong to men in Christ. He gives thanks for God's election of men from eternity to be his children,—an election of which it is to be observed that, as the fact and character of it are seen wholly in Christ and not in men, it cannot be restricted by any limits which are not to be discerned in Christ, and that therefore it must be understood as going forth from the inherently gracious Will of God towards mankind generally; for the deliverance of men through forgiveness from that bondage of sin which separates them from God; for the revelation of God's grand purpose, to make Christ the one Head of an obedient creation; for the special inheritance of sonship promised to faithful men, of which the filial Spirit already given was the earnest.

In the second paragraph, the thanksgiving changes to a prayer, that the readers of the Epistle may have their eyes opened to the blessings for which thanks had been given; and especially, that they might know that *power*, which had wrought in the raising and exaltation of Christ, and which, as the putting forth of one and the same will, was working upon all believers.

Yes, the Apostle goes on to say, the resurrection and exaltation of Christ were the quickening from the death of sin, and the exalting to a heavenly sphere of existence, of his members with him. Those who believed in Christ were actually inspired with a new life and raised above the world and the dark powers of the world. This was God's act, *a part*, it might be said, *of the same act* which wrought in Christ. Man could only receive and submit; the only good deeds which he could do were such as were prepared for him beforehand by the design and power of his Maker.

The next paragraph (ii. 11—22) presents a new aspect of what had been done for mankind in Christ. To a Jewish eye the world had been divided by the exclusive call of the seed of Abraham into two separate sections. When the Son of God appeared, taking the flesh and blood of humanity upon him, representing the human race in the sight of the Father, offering himself a sacrifice for all, entering into the death of all, fulfilling the promise that in the seed of Abraham all the nations of the earth should be blessed, the separation was done away. The human race became one body, united in one Head, reconciled to one Father, animated by one filial and brotherly Spirit. The Gentiles, having been formerly destitute of the peculiar Jewish privileges, were now made partakers with the Jews of blessings which the old Jewish privileges had but faintly foreshadowed.

The Apostle's heart now swells with the contemplation of these spiritual glories (c. iii.). A touching humility and tenderness take possession of him as he thinks how unspeakably he has himself been honoured in being made the herald of this union of all men in the family of God. What a revelation of hidden things had that age received! O that all might be spiritually wrought upon to fulfil through faith and love the grand idea of the Maker, to the glory of the Father through Christ!

The eucharistic declaration of Christian privileges being thus closed, St. Paul begins the Second Part of the Epistle, which contains lessons of duty founded on those privileges. But the eucharistic *feeling* does not at once subside; the more level movement of practical exhortation is still lifted, as it were, by a kind of ground-swell of spiritual emotion. The first paragraph (iv. 1—16) is rather declaratory than hortatory. It speaks of unity,—the unity which God has ordained in Christ, and which men may *keep* by modesty and forbearance, and by the abiding of each in his own place. We are reminded that there is an organization of the Christian Society on earth which represents and ministers to the higher heavenly unity. The ideal unity of the Church (set forth under the favourite Pauline image of a full-grown Man, with Christ as the Head) is to be realized through truth and love. In the succeeding paragraph (ii. 17—32) the new Divinely-given life is placed in contrast with the old corrupt life. The Apostle conjures his Christian readers to put away practically the evil which in profession they had renounced, and to clothe themselves with all the virtues which belonged to their calling in Christ.

It is the strict dependence of all that is commended as practical duty upon the calling or status of men in Christ, that is to be specially noticed in the exhortations which follow (v., vi. 1—9). God is to be imitated as a Father, by those whom he has made his children. The new kingdom must have *obedient* subjects. Light must bring forth its fruits in those who have become children of light. The Spirit must manifest his presence in the body by the tokens of inspiration. The relations of husband and wife, parents and children, masters and servants, are sacred, and are to be mutually fulfilled in obedience to Christ.

The concluding appeal or peroration (vi. 10—20), breathing a very lofty and eloquent tone, contains a carefully-wrought account of the warfare between the Church and the powers of darkness and evil which brood over the world. It is to be observed that here, as generally throughout the Apostolic writings, the imagery is borrowed from the poetical books of the Old Testament. Most of it may be found in the book of Isaiah. The warfare described is not the battle of the individual Christian for his own salvation, but the greater conflict in which Christ leads his forces against the enemy, the war of the Gospel against the powers which keep mankind in slavery. But individual Christians are the soldiers in this war, and the armour mentioned is such as individual Christians must put on.

The sentences with which the Epistle closes,—the mention and commendation of the messenger who was to carry it, and the usual benedictory prayer,—remind us that this was a *bonâ fide* pastoral letter, addressed to Christians who looked up to St. Paul as their teacher.

ΠΡΟΣ ΕΦΕΣΙΟΥΣ.

I. 1 Παῦλος ἀπόστολος Χριστοῦ Ἰησοῦ διὰ θελήματος θεοῦ τοῖς ἁγίοις τοῖς οὖσιν [ἐν Ἐφέσῳ] καὶ πιστοῖς 2 ἐν Χριστῷ Ἰησοῦ. χάρις ὑμῖν καὶ εἰρήνη ἀπὸ θεοῦ πατρὸς ἡμῶν καὶ κυρίου Ἰησοῦ Χριστοῦ.

3 Εὐλογητὸς ὁ θεὸς καὶ πατὴρ τοῦ κυρίου ἡμῶν

1. ἐν Ἐφέσῳ. There is sufficient evidence to throw a doubt upon the genuineness of these words. St. Basil and St. Jerome speak of their being omitted in some ancient MSS.; and two of the most important MSS. which have come down to us, the Sinaitic and the Vatican, do not contain them in the writing of the first hand. It is impossible to believe that the sentence was intended to be complete without the mention of any place after τοῖς οὖσιν. The suggestion that τοῖς ἁγίοις τοῖς οὖσιν may be rendered "the saints who *are*," with an allusion to their partaking of the substantial existence of "Him who *is*," does not call for serious consideration. The omission of ἐν Ἐφέσῳ in some ancient MSS. must be understood to point, either to an early doubt as to the readers to whom the Epistle was addressed, or, it may be, to an original blank filled up variously in different copies, which were sent to different Churches. See the Introduction, p. 12.

ἐν Χριστῷ Ἰησοῦ. Christ is named as the bond of the believers; "the holy and faithful community in Christ Jesus." Compare the salutations to the Philippians and Colossians.

3. For the subject of this paragraph, see the Introduction, p. 23.

ὁ θεὸς καὶ πατὴρ τοῦ κ . . . "Blessed be God and the Father of . . ." That is, "He who is God and the Father of . . ." This seems to be a more natural rendering, whilst it is not less accurate, than that of our Version, "the God and Father of our Lord." The latter, however, has the support of the similar expression in verse 17.

Ἰησοῦ Χριστοῦ, ὁ εὐλογήσας ἡμᾶς ἐν πάσῃ εὐλογίᾳ
4 πνευματικῇ ἐν τοῖς ἐπουρανίοις ἐν Χριστῷ, καθὼς
ἐξελέξατο ἡμᾶς ἐν αὐτῷ πρὸ καταβολῆς κόσμου, εἶναι
ἡμᾶς ἁγίους καὶ ἀμώμους κατενώπιον αὐτοῦ, ἐν ἀγάπῃ
5 προορίσας ἡμᾶς εἰς υἱοθεσίαν διὰ Ἰησοῦ Χριστοῦ
εἰς αὐτόν, κατὰ τὴν εὐδοκίαν τοῦ θελήματος αὐτοῦ,
6 εἰς ἔπαινον δόξης τῆς χάριτος αὐτοῦ, ἐν ᾗ ἐχαρί-
7 τωσεν ἡμᾶς ἐν τῷ ἠγαπημένῳ, ἐν ᾧ ἔχομεν τὴν
ἀπολύτρωσιν διὰ τοῦ αἵματος αὐτοῦ, τὴν ἄφεσιν τῶν
παραπτωμάτων, κατὰ τὸ πλοῦτος τῆς χάριτος αὐτοῦ,
8 ἧς ἐπερίσσευσεν εἰς ἡμᾶς ἐν πάσῃ σοφίᾳ καὶ φρο-
9 νήσει γνωρίσας ἡμῖν τὸ μυστήριον τοῦ θελήματος

ἐν τοῖς ἐπουρανίοις, "in the heavenly world or sphere," "in spiritual relations." There is no reference to place or to a future time.

4. As to the scope of this election, see the remark in the Introduction, p. 23.

ἐν ἀγάπῃ. I have not thought it worth while to alter in the translation the received connexion of the words "in love." By placing the comma *before* them, Lachmann and Tischendorf connect them with God's act of foreordaining, and in making the former clause end with αὐτοῦ they have the support of the clause in Col. i. 22, παραστῆσαι ὑμᾶς ἁγίους καὶ ἀμώμους καὶ ἀνεγκλήτους. Either arrangement is so satisfactory, that the one cannot be very decidedly preferred to the other.

6. τῆς χάριτος αὐτοῦ, ἐν ᾗ [or ἧς. Lach.] ἐχαρίτωσεν ἡμᾶς. Most literally, "the grace with which he has graced us;" "the grace which he has freely bestowed upon us." The uncommon verb ἐχαρίτωσεν is used in order to repeat the idea of χάρις.

7. The redemption of men, or their deliverance from bondage by the payment of a price, is explained as consisting in the remission or forgiveness of sins. He who really receives the forgiveness of sins is thereby made spiritually free. The blood of Christ was the cost of the deliverance, because Christ gave his life in order that men might be reconciled to God.

9. γνωρίσας should be closely connected with ἐπερίσσευσεν. God abounded... *when he made known* ... The abounding of God towards us in wisdom and prudence was exhibited in his making known to us the mystery of his will. The

I. 10—13.] EPISTLE TO THE EPHESIANS. 29

αὐτοῦ, κατὰ τὴν εὐδοκίαν αὐτοῦ ἣν προέθετο ἐν
10 αὐτῷ εἰς οἰκονομίαν τοῦ πληρώματος τῶν καιρῶν,
ἀνακεφαλαιώσασθαι τὰ πάντα ἐν τῷ Χριστῷ, τὰ ἐν
11 τοῖς οὐρανοῖς καὶ τὰ ἐπὶ τῆς γῆς, ἐν αὐτῷ ἐν ᾧ καὶ
ἐκληρώθημεν προορισθέντες κατὰ πρόθεσιν τοῦ τὰ
πάντα ἐνεργοῦντος κατὰ τὴν βουλὴν τοῦ θελήματος
12 αὐτοῦ, εἰς τὸ εἶναι ἡμᾶς εἰς ἔπαινον δόξης αὐτοῦ,
13 τοὺς προηλπικότας ἐν τῷ Χριστῷ· ἐν ᾧ καὶ ὑμεῖς,
ἀκούσαντες τὸν λόγον τῆς ἀληθείας, τὸ εὐαγγέλιον

Apostle affirms here, as he does elsewhere, that the whole purpose of God revealed in Christ was a subject of inexhaustible study for the intellect.

10. εἰς οἰκονομίαν τοῦ πληρώματος τῶν καιρῶν. The word οἰκονομία, a favourite one with St. Paul, is used by him in three distinct senses. (1) It is God's plan or arrangement, the Divine order to be accomplished in Christ. We may render it "dispensation" in this sense, or use it in its English form *economy*. This is its meaning here, and probably in iii. 9. (2) It represents an appointment or commission given by the Lord to his servant Paul, in Eph. iii. 2, and in Col. i. 25. Δωρεά is used in Eph. iii. 7, as nearly an equivalent to this sense of οἰκονομία,—the most frequent word however for this commission being χάρις. In these two cases the οἰκόνομος is God or Christ. (3) It represents a stewardship. So, perhaps, in iii. 9. In 1 Cor. iv. 1, 2, St. Paul describes himself as an οἰκόνομος, having the duty of dispensing, or giving out to others, the mysteries entrusted to him.

God's purpose in Christ had reference "to the dispensation of [belonging to] the fulness of the times." Compare Gal. iv. 4, "When the fulness of the time was come, God sent forth his Son." This economy, or dispensation, or system of things, which the purpose of God contemplated from eternity, is "the bringing of all things under one head in Christ." ἀνακεφαλαιώσασθαι, to sum up, to gather under a head.

11. ἐκληρώθημεν, "obtained a lot, or inheritance." Another reading, ἐκλήθημεν, is strongly supported by MS. authority, and is introduced into the text by Lachmann.

12. τοὺς προηλπικότας. The only sense which can here be given to προ- in this word seems to be that of our Version, "who were first or forward to hope in Christ."

τῆς σωτηρίας ὑμῶν, ἐν ᾧ καὶ πιστεύσαντες ἐσφρα-
14 γίσθητε τῷ πνεύματι τῆς ἐπαγγελίας τῷ ἁγίῳ, ὅς
ἐστιν ἀρραβὼν τῆς κληρονομίας ἡμῶν εἰς ἀπολύτρωσιν τῆς περιποιήσεως, εἰς ἔπαινον τῆς δόξης αὐτοῦ.
15 Διὰ τοῦτο κἀγώ, ἀκούσας τὴν καθ᾽ ὑμᾶς πίστιν

13. *ἐν ᾧ καὶ ὑμεῖς, ... ἐν ᾧ καὶ πιστεύσαντες.* The words *ἐν ᾧ* appear to be *repeated* for the sake of perspicuity before *πιστεύσαντες*. If we omit these words, the sentence proceeds with grammatical smoothness: "in whom you also, when you had heard the word of truth, the gospel of your salvation, and had believed, or become believers, were sealed." The "hearing" and "believing" are connected: "faith cometh by hearing."

The Spirit of promise is the promised Spirit. Compare Acts i. 4, "wait for the promise of the Father which you heard from me." The *sealing* with the Spirit means the actual outpouring of the Spirit, such as took place when converts were introduced into the Church, which answered to sealing, because it was a recognizable stamp of Divine ownership. Compare iv. 30, and 2 Cor. i. 22, "God hath also sealed us, and given us the earnest of the Spirit in our hearts."

14. The gift of the Spirit, besides being a seal which marked those who received it as belonging to God, was also, as a seal of *sonship*, an earnest or pledge of a future *inheritance*. "If children, then heirs." In time the believers in Christ shall come into the full possession of the inheritance of sons of God. At present, the perfect blessedness of sonship is given them in prospect rather than in possession. But they hold already, in the pouring out of the Spirit of sonship, an earnest *εἰς ἀπολύτρωσιν τῆς περιποιήσεως*, a pledge pointing to the complete acquisition of the property. The "property" is whatever belongs to the nature and functions of sons of God. The "redemption" here is that of the property; and the figure must not be pressed too closely. On the other hand, in iv. 30, "unto the day of redemption," we should naturally take it as referring to the setting free of the human nature; especially as in Romans viii. 16—23, an important passage to compare with these, the filial adoption is said to be accomplished in the "redemption of our *body*." But, as the use of *οἰκονομία*, of *πλήρωμα*, and other words, shews us, St. Paul varies much in the application even of favourite and highly significant terms.

15. For the subject of this paragraph see the Introduction, p. 23.

ἐν τῷ κυρίῳ Ἰησοῦ καὶ τὴν ἀγάπην τὴν εἰς πάντας
16 τοὺς ἁγίους, οὐ παύομαι εὐχαριστῶν ὑπὲρ ὑμῶν,
17 μνείαν ὑμῶν ποιούμενος ἐπὶ τῶν προσευχῶν μου, ἵνα
ὁ θεὸς τοῦ κυρίου ἡμῶν Ἰησοῦ Χριστοῦ, ὁ πατὴρ
τῆς δόξης, δῴη ὑμῖν πνεῦμα σοφίας καὶ ἀποκαλύ-
18 ψεως ἐν ἐπιγνώσει αὐτοῦ, πεφωτισμένους τοὺς ὀφ-
θαλμοὺς τῆς καρδίας ὑμῶν, εἰς τὸ εἰδέναι ὑμᾶς τίς
ἐστιν ἡ ἐλπὶς τῆς κλήσεως αὐτοῦ, καὶ τίς ὁ πλοῦτος
19 τῆς δόξης τῆς κληρονομίας αὐτοῦ ἐν τοῖς ἁγίοις, καὶ
τί τὸ ὑπερβάλλον μέγεθος τῆς δυνάμεως αὐτοῦ εἰς
ἡμᾶς τοὺς πιστεύοντας κατὰ τὴν ἐνέργειαν τοῦ κρά-
20 τους τῆς ἰσχύος αὐτοῦ, ἣν ἐνήργησεν ἐν τῷ Χριστῷ

15, 16. Compare Col. i. 3, 4, and Phil. 4, 5.

17. ἵνα, "to the effect that;" what follows being the *purport* of the prayer, and not merely its aim or end.

πνεῦμα ἀποκαλύψεως, "a spirit of revelation,"—the spirit whose influences may remove the veil which hides invisible realities from the soul.

18. πεφωτισμένους ὀφθαλμούς. The accusative is owing to the influence of δῴη. For the sense, compare 1 Cor. ii. 9—12.

ἡ ἐλπὶς τῆς κλήσεως αὐτοῦ, "the hope held out in his calling," the whole promise set before believers in Christ.

τῆς κληρονομίας αὐτοῦ ἐν τοῖς ἁγίοις. What is "God's inheritance" here? It might mean either the inheritance of which he himself takes possession, or that which he gives. The latter sense is the more obvious one, and agrees better with the expressions concerning inheritance so frequent in St. Paul's writings. But the words ἐν τοῖς ἁγίοις almost demand the former sense. God (in Christ) has an inheritance in the body of the saints. Those whose eyes are opened may see how rich is the glory of the redeemed community, how bright is that perfect creation of which Christ is the inheritor.

19. τοὺς πιστεύοντας, "towards us believers,"—not to be construed with κατὰ τὴν ἐνέργειαν.

20. ἣν ἐνήργησεν, "*with* which he wrought," ἣν being in the accusative to agree with τὴν ἐνέργειαν. ἐκάθισεν is to be coupled, somewhat irregularly, with ἐνήργησεν. If καθίσας, for which there is good authority, be read, it is coupled with ἐγείρας. Observe particularly the identification of that energy of God which

ἐγείρας αὐτὸν ἐκ νεκρῶν, καὶ ἐκάθισεν ἐν δεξιᾷ
21 αὐτοῦ ἐν τοῖς ἐπουρανίοις ὑπεράνω πάσης ἀρχῆς καὶ
ἐξουσίας καὶ δυνάμεως καὶ κυριότητος καὶ παντὸς
ὀνόματος ὀνομαζομένου οὐ μόνον ἐν τῷ αἰῶνι τούτῳ

wrought in the raising and exalting of Christ with the energy that works continuously on the body of which he was raised to be the Head. (Compare "the power that works in us," iii. 20.) Christ is not apart from the Church in the Divine idea, any more than the Church is apart from Christ.

21. We need not define or distinguish what is meant by these terms. They are accumulated so as to be all-embracing and exhaustive. Compare the quotations from Philo and the Avesta in the *Essay*.

οὐ μόνον ἐν τῷ αἰῶνι τούτῳ ἀλλὰ καὶ ἐν τῷ μέλλοντι. The right interpretation of these terms forms one of the principal difficulties of the New Testament. The same expressions occur in Matt. xii. 32, "Whosoever shall speak against the Holy Ghost, it shall not be forgiven him, either in this age or in that which is to come." In Matt. xiii. 39, 40, Jesus refers to "the end or conclusion (συντέλεια) of the age." The discourse of Matt. xxiv. and xxv. is introduced by the question, "What shall be the sign of thy coming and of the end or conclusion of the age?" In Heb. vi. 5, we have the remarkable expression "have tasted the good word of God and *the powers of the coming age*." Apparently the word οἰκουμένη, *world*, is used as equivalent to αἰών in Heb. ii. 5, "It is not to angels that he has subjected the world to come, of which we speak." In 1 Cor. x. 11, the age which is closing becomes plural, "the ends of the ages," ἡμῶν εἰς οὓς τὰ τέλη τῶν αἰώνων κατήντηκεν. In Eph. ii. 7, the *future* age becomes plural, ἐν τοῖς αἰῶσιν τοῖς ἐπερχομένοις. And in Eph. iii. 21, we have the redoubled phrase, "unto all the generations of the age of ages."

Thus much may be said with confidence as to the meaning of this New Testament language. The Apostles believed, after the teaching of their Lord, that in their day a great αἰών or Age was drawing to a close; and that in a short time, by a crisis in the Divine administration of the world, described as a Coming of the Son of Man, a new Age or succession of ages would be inaugurated. Were they mistaken? It is usual to say that they *were*;—naturally and even advantageously mistaken. But before using so strong a word as 'mistaken,' we should be sure both that we

22 ἀλλὰ καὶ ἐν τῷ μέλλοντι, καὶ πάντα ὑπέταξεν ὑπὸ τοὺς πόδας αὐτοῦ, καὶ αὐτὸν ἔδωκεν κεφαλὴν ὑπὲρ
23 πάντα τῇ ἐκκλησίᾳ, ἥτις ἐστὶν τὸ σῶμα αὐτοῦ, τὸ πλήρωμα τοῦ τὰ πάντα ἐν πᾶσιν πληρουμένου.

rightly understand the intention of their language, and also that we adequately estimate the magnitude, from a Christian point of view, of the revolution which took place at the epoch of the destruction of Jerusalem.

22. πάντα ὑπέταξεν. Compare Psa. viii. 6, Heb. ii. 8, and 1 Cor. xv. 27. We see not yet all things put under Christ's feet, because the appointed order is not yet victorious over disobedience. But in the mind of God all things are even now put under the feet of Christ.

23. τὸ πλήρωμα τοῦ τὰ πάντα ἐν πᾶσιν πληρουμένου. Πλήρωμα here means *complement*. In iii. 19, and iv. 13, it rather means *completeness*. In the Epistle to the Colossians (i. 19, ii. 9) it is used absolutely for the Infinite Fulness, as a title of God. The Church is here called the πλήρωμα of Christ, because he would not be "full" or complete without it. The rest of the clause is difficult to render with precision. The reduplicative phrases, fold over fold, in which St. Paul delights, are not only not easy to translate, but they are often somewhat obscure and ambiguous in meaning. Does St. Paul mean anything more here than if he had written τοῦ τὰ πάντα πληροῦντος (as in iv. 10, ἵνα πληρώσῃ τὰ πάντα)?—As regards the use of the middle form πληρουμένου, we may perhaps say, from the analogy of πληροῦσθαι ναῦν, "to man one's ship," that it suggests the idea of Christ's filling *what belongs to him*. Ἐν πᾶσιν is coupled with τὰ πάντα in Col. iii. 11, τὰ πάντα καὶ ἐν πᾶσιν Χριστός, and in 1 Cor. xii. 6, ὁ αὐτὸς θεὸς ὁ ἐνεργῶν τὰ πάντα ἐν πᾶσιν. In these places πᾶσιν refers not to things, but to men. The hint thus given, that ἐν πᾶσιν may have the same reference here, derives some support from the consideration that the subject of the sentence is Christ's body the Church, and from the expressions ἵνα πληρωθῆτε εἰς πᾶν τὸ πλήρωμα τοῦ θεοῦ (iii. 19), πληροῦσθε ἐν πνεύματι (v. 18), and ἐστε ἐν αὐτῷ πεπληρωμένοι (Col. ii. 10). If ἐν πᾶσιν is "in all (men)," we must understand St. Paul as blending the thoughts that Christ is in all and that he fills all things. The Church is "the fulness of him who in all is the filler of all things." Possibly however it may be only meant that Christ fills all things *everywhere*.

Passages from Philo concerning

II. 1 Καὶ ὑμᾶς ὄντας νεκροὺς τοῖς παραπτώμασιν καὶ
2 ταῖς ἁμαρτίαις, ἐν αἷς ποτὲ περιεπατήσατε κατὰ τὸν
αἰῶνα τοῦ κόσμου τούτου, κατὰ τὸν ἄρχοντα τῆς
ἐξουσίας τοῦ ἀέρος, τοῦ πνεύματος τοῦ νῦν ἐνερ-
3 γοῦντος ἐν τοῖς υἱοῖς τῆς ἀπειθείας, ἐν οἷς καὶ ἡμεῖς
πάντες ἀνεστράφημέν ποτε ἐν ταῖς ἐπιθυμίαις τῆς
σαρκὸς ἡμῶν, ποιοῦντες τὰ θελήματα τῆς σαρκὸς καὶ
τῶν διανοιῶν, καὶ ἦμεν τέκνα φύσει ὀργῆς ὡς καὶ οἱ

God as filling all things are given in the *Essay*.

II. 1. The quickening of the Ephesian Christians was an example of that power of life which wrought in raising Christ from the dead. Ὑμᾶς was evidently to be governed by some word meaning "he has raised to life." Συνεζωοποίησεν does occur further on, after the construction has been broken.

2. κατὰ τὸν αἰῶνα. We can hardly do better than render αἰών as in our E. V., "the course." Moral or historical features are implied in the term αἰών.

κατὰ τὸν ἄρχοντα τῆς ἐξουσίας τοῦ ἀέρος, τοῦ πνεύματος ... τῆς ἀπειθείας. Compare vi. 12, πρὸς τοὺς κοσμοκράτορας τοῦ σκότους τούτου, πρὸς τὰ πνευματικὰ τῆς πονηρίας ἐν τοῖς ἐπουρανίοις. These remarkable terms appear to be carefully chosen. They aim at describing a certain mysterious power, diffused in the air, ruling in, and by means of, spiritual darkness brooding over the earth.

There is no reason to doubt that St. Paul would have used the names Σατανᾶς and διάβολος, Enemy and Divider, to denote the same power. But in choosing such words as the above, and in using the singular and the plural alternately (τὸν ἄρχοντα, τοὺς κοσμοκράτορας), it is probable that the Apostle was seeking to portray a less defined and more subtle agency than a personal name is apt to suggest. As to the genitive τοῦ πνεύματος, it is just possible to take τοῦ πνεύματος as in apposition to either ἐξουσίας or ἀέρος and governed by ἄρχοντα, but it is simpler and more natural to believe that the Apostle would have written τὸ πνεῦμα in the accusative but for the "attraction" of the preceding genitives, and that the "ruler" *is*, rather than governs, "the spirit." Compare the language of the Avesta concerning Angro-mainyus and the Daevas, quoted in the *Essay*.

3. τῶν διανοιῶν, the thoughts, or the mind.

ἦμεν τέκνα φύσει ὀργῆς, "were

4 λοιποί· ὁ δὲ θεὸς πλούσιος ὢν ἐν ἐλέει, διὰ τὴν
5 πολλὴν ἀγάπην αὐτοῦ ἣν ἠγάπησεν ἡμᾶς, καὶ ὄντας
ἡμᾶς νεκροὺς τοῖς παραπτώμασιν συνεζωοποίησεν τῷ
6 Χριστῷ, χάριτί ἐστε σεσωσμένοι, καὶ συνήγειρεν καὶ
συνεκάθισεν ἐν τοῖς ἐπουρανίοις ἐν Χριστῷ Ἰησοῦ,
7 ἵνα ἐνδείξηται ἐν τοῖς αἰῶσιν τοῖς ἐπερχομένοις τὸ
ὑπερβάλλον πλοῦτος τῆς χάριτος αὐτοῦ ἐν χρηστότητι
8 ἐφ' ἡμᾶς ἐν Χριστῷ Ἰησοῦ. τῇ γὰρ χάριτί ἐστε
σεσωσμένοι διὰ τῆς πίστεως, καὶ τοῦτο οὐκ ἐξ ὑμῶν,
9 θεοῦ τὸ δῶρον· οὐκ ἐξ ἔργων, ἵνα μή τις καυχήσηται·

children, by nature, of wrath." It is a tempting interpretation, on account of its great suitableness to the context, to take ὀργή in its original sense, of "passion" or animal impulse, and τέκνα ὀργῆς as "children of ungoverned impulse." But St. Paul's habitual use of ὀργή, and the closely parallel passage in this Epistle (v. 6), "On account of these things comes the wrath (ὀργή) of God on the sons of disobedience," compel us to take this phrase in the commonly received sense,—that of "children of Divine wrath," persons, who through submission to the flesh, which is enmity against God, lie under God's anger.

5, 6. If it is asked *when* these Divine acts were done, the answer must be, that they were done when Christ himself was raised and exalted, and that they were then done because of the necessary and indissoluble connexion between the Head and his members,—the Divine power which wrought in him descending also (i. 19—23) upon them. (Compare Col. ii. 12, 13; iii. 1—5.) But the living fellowship in a new and heavenly existence between Christ and men, which was then originally and ideally organized, is practically and gradually carried out through the faith of Christ's members in him, and in proportion to their faith. This takes place ἐν τοῖς αἰῶσιν τοῖς ἐπερχομένοις (ver. 7).

5, 8. χάριτί ἐστε σεσωσμένοι. St. Paul assumes that his readers had already been raised to that fellowship with Christ risen and exalted, to be in which is to be "saved." This salvation was due to God's grace, and wrought out by faith.

καὶ τοῦτο. Additional emphasis is laid upon the Divine origin of salvation. St. Paul was afraid that even salvation by grace through faith might be referred to some primary source in human

10 αὐτοῦ γάρ ἐσμεν ποίημα, κτισθέντες ἐν Χριστῷ Ἰησοῦ
ἐπὶ ἔργοις ἀγαθοῖς οἷς προητοίμασεν ὁ θεὸς ἵνα ἐν
αὐτοῖς περιπατήσωμεν.

11 Διὸ μνημονεύετε ὅτι ποτὲ ὑμεῖς τὰ ἔθνη ἐν σαρκί,
οἱ λεγόμενοι ἀκροβυστία ὑπὸ τῆς λεγομένης περι-
12 τομῆς ἐν σαρκὶ χειροποιήτου, ὅτι ἦτε τῷ καιρῷ
ἐκείνῳ χωρὶς Χριστοῦ ἀπηλλοτριωμένοι τῆς πολιτείας

nature; so he adds, "And that not of, or from, yourselves,—the gift is God's,—not of works," that is, not primarily from any human devices.

10. ἐπὶ ἔργοις ἀγαθοῖς. Although not ἐξ ἔργων, yet ἐπὶ ἔργοις,—an unusual but significant use of ἐπί followed by a dative. It implies a certain basis or condition. We are created in Christ Jesus upon a certain hypothesis, as it were, or plan, of good works to be done by us. Does this act of creation belong to the commencement of our natural existence, or to that of our Christian life?—Not exactly to either, but to the Divine mind or purpose, in the fiat of which each kind of existence originates. Compare iv. 24; Col. iii. 10.

11. For the subject of this paragraph, see the Introduction, p. 23.

12. In reminding the Gentiles of what they had formerly been, the Apostle intends to contrast their condition, point by point, with that of the Jews. Each negative statement as to the Gentiles implies a corresponding privilege which had belonged to the Jews. Thus the Jews had had their national existence associated with that of a Messiah; they had been constituted into a Commonwealth founded upon covenants of promise; they had had a distinct hope held out before them; a God had revealed himself to them in their world. In all these respects the Gentiles had been formerly at a disadvantage compared with the Jews. They had been χωρὶς Χριστοῦ,—not, unvisited by the Light which enlightens every man, but without a Christ, unassociated with the Messiah of whom the Jewish prophets bore witness. Whatever advantages of unity and life the Jews had possessed in their Divinely-organized Commonwealth and in the covenanted Promise on which they depended, were wanting to the Gentiles. ἐλπίδα μὴ ἔχοντες καὶ ἄθεοι ἐν τῷ κόσμῳ, "not having a Hope (as the Jews had), and without a God (revealed like Jehovah) in the world." The world had indeed been full of gods (gods

τοῦ Ἰσραὴλ καὶ ξένοι τῶν διαθηκῶν τῆς ἐπαγγελίας,
13 ἐλπίδα μὴ ἔχοντες καὶ ἄθεοι ἐν τῷ κόσμῳ· νυνὶ δὲ
ἐν Χριστῷ Ἰησοῦ ὑμεῖς οἵ ποτε ὄντες μακρὰν ἐγγὺς
14 ἐγενήθητε ἐν τῷ αἵματι τοῦ Χριστοῦ. αὐτὸς γάρ
ἐστιν ἡ εἰρήνη ἡμῶν, ὁ ποιήσας τὰ ἀμφότερα ἓν καὶ
15 τὸ μεσότοιχον τοῦ φραγμοῦ λύσας, τὴν ἔχθραν, ἐν
τῇ σαρκὶ αὐτοῦ τὸν νόμον τῶν ἐντολῶν ἐν δόγμασιν
καταργήσας, ἵνα τοὺς δύο κτίσῃ ἐν ἑαυτῷ εἰς ἕνα

many and lords many, in heaven and in earth) to the Gentile. But the Apostle could not take these into account by the side of Jehovah the God of his fathers; and, such as they were, they had almost disappeared in that age.

"The intelligible forms of ancient poets,
The fair humanities of old religion,
The Power, the Beauty, and the Majesty,
That had their haunts in dale, or piny mountain,
Or forest by slow stream, or pebbly spring,
Or chasms, and watery depths; all these had vanished."

The world was not the world of a Living God to the Gentile races.

13. Νυνὶ δέ. But now this is all changed. The separation has given place to union in the same privileges infinitely enhanced.

ἐν τῷ αἵματι τοῦ Χριστοῦ. The blood, the flesh, the sacrifice, the person, of Christ, are become the means of uniting together the divided parts of humanity, because in him humanity as a whole is reconciled and united to God.

14. τὸ μεσότοιχον τοῦ φραγμοῦ,
"the dividing-wall or fence of the enclosure," within which the Jews were kept apart from the Gentiles.

14, 15. τὴν ἔχθραν. The comma after ἔχθραν is better omitted. In accordance with the general thought of this passage, "the enmity" like the "peace" is twofold, between man and God, and between Jews and Gentiles. And the enmity is represented by *the Law*, "the law of commandments in decrees." Similarly in Col. ii. 14, "the handwriting in decrees" is said to have been "adverse to us;" τὸ καθ' ἡμῶν χειρόγραφον τοῖς δόγμασιν ὃ ἦν ὑπεναντίον ἡμῖν. The Jewish Law was only an example of the general principle of Law, of which it is the nature, according to St. Paul, to enjoin with absolute authority all that is right, without giving to the weak and perverse will any power to do it. The effect of Law therefore, as embodied in δόγματα or decrees, was to condemn, and so to drive away from God. Both Jews and Gentiles were subject to this influence of Law, and being thereby

16 καινὸν ἄνθρωπον ποιῶν εἰρήνην, καὶ ἀποκαταλλάξῃ
τοὺς ἀμφοτέρους ἐν ἑνὶ σώματι τῷ θεῷ διὰ τοῦ
17 σταυροῦ, ἀποκτείνας τὴν ἔχθραν ἐν αὐτῷ. καὶ ἐλθὼν
εὐηγγελίσατο εἰρήνην ὑμῖν τοῖς μακρὰν καὶ εἰρήνην
18 τοῖς ἐγγύς, ὅτι δι' αὐτοῦ ἔχομεν τὴν προσαγωγὴν οἱ
19 ἀμφότεροι ἐν ἑνὶ πνεύματι πρὸς τὸν πατέρα. Ἄρα
οὖν οὐκέτι ἐστὲ ξένοι καὶ πάροικοι, ἀλλ' ἐστὲ συμπο-
20 λῖται τῶν ἁγίων καὶ οἰκεῖοι τοῦ θεοῦ, ἐποικοδομη-
θέντες ἐπὶ τῷ θεμελίῳ τῶν ἀποστόλων καὶ προφητῶν,
21 ὄντος ἀκρογωνιαίου αὐτοῦ Χριστοῦ Ἰησοῦ, ἐν ᾧ πᾶσα

separated from God were also necessarily kept from peace amongst themselves; whilst the Jewish Law was further a symbol and agent of separation between Jews and Gentiles. For the Law, as seen in decrees only, Jesus Christ substituted *himself*, dying a sacrifice to God for men, and thus established a bond of love and life between the Father and the hearts of men.

17. ἐλθὼν εὐηγγελίσατο. The coming and the proclaiming of glad tidings might be taken as referring in general to the whole advent of the Son of God in the flesh. But the Apostles were accustomed to speak of their Lord as having " come " on the Day of Pentecost and as preaching glad tidings and peace by the mouth of his ambassadors. " Unto you first God, *having raised up* his Son Jesus, *sent him* to bless you" (Acts iii. 26). " I will not leave you comfortless; I will come to you. Yet a little while, and the world seeth me no more; but ye see me" (St. John xiv. 18, 19).

19. What the Gentiles are now, in contrast with what they were (verse 12).

οἰκεῖοι τοῦ θεοῦ, " members of God's household." Compare τοὺς οἰκείους τῆς πίστεως, Gal. vi. 10. God's house is large enough for many inmates; Christ has prepared places in it for all believers (St. John xiv. 2, 3).

20. ἐπὶ τῷ θεμελίῳ τῶν ἀποστόλων καὶ προφητῶν. The apostles and prophets are the foundation of the Church, as being the first stones laid upon the common foundation of all, and as drawing by their testimony other believers who were laid as stones upon them. St. Peter was the first stone, (Πέτρος, Κηφᾶς,) through his first confession of Jesus as the Son of the Living God. Compare 1 Pet. ii. 4, 5; Rev. xxi. 14. The prophets are not those of the Old

οἰκοδομὴ συναρμολογουμένη αὔξει εἰς ναὸν ἅγιον ἐν 22 κυρίῳ, ἐν ᾧ καὶ ὑμεῖς συνοικοδομεῖσθε εἰς κατοικητήριον τοῦ θεοῦ ἐν πνεύματι.

III. 1 Τούτου χάριν ἐγὼ Παῦλος ὁ δέσμιος τοῦ Χριστοῦ 2 Ἰησοῦ ὑπὲρ ὑμῶν τῶν ἐθνῶν εἴ γε ἠκούσατε τὴν οἰκονομίαν τῆς χάριτος τοῦ θεοῦ τῆς δοθείσης μοι εἰς 3 ὑμᾶς, ὅτι κατὰ ἀποκάλυψιν ἐγνωρίσθη μοι τὸ μυστή- 4 ριον, καθὼς προέγραψα ἐν ὀλίγῳ, πρὸς ὃ δύνασθε

Covenant, but the teachers associated with the Apostles of Christ, as in iii. 5; iv. 11; 1 Cor. xii. 28.

ἀκρογωνιαίου. See Isa. xxviii. 16; Ps. cxviii. 22; Matt. xxi. 42.

III. 1. Τούτου χάριν. The reference is to the whole preceding statement of the Christian calling and condition, which serves as a reason for the vows and exhortations which are now to be poured forth. The sentence is interrupted after verse 1, and resumed at verse 14.

ὁ δέσμιος τοῦ Χριστοῦ Ἰησοῦ ὑπὲρ ὑμῶν τῶν ἐθνῶν. St. Paul cherished his imprisonment as a mark of honourable service under his Master. His whole life was "on behalf of the Gentiles;" but the imprisonment was expressly due to his faithfulness in maintaining their right to all the privileges of the Gospel. Compare Acts xxi. xxii. especially xxii. 21, 22.

2. τὴν οἰκονομίαν τῆς χάριτος, "the dispensation of the grace." οἰκονομία is a system of management. The meaning of the phrase here is nearly this: "If you have heard of the grace, which, *under God's providence*, has been given me towards you." χάρις, a grace or favour, is habitually used by St. Paul to denote his Apostolic vocation. See verses 7, 8; Gal. ii. 9; Philip. i. 7; Rom. i. 4; xii. 3; xv. 15; 1 Cor. iii. 10; xv. 10. οἰκονομία is used by itself in Col. i. 25, κατὰ τὴν οἰκονομίαν τοῦ θεοῦ τὴν δοθεῖσάν μοι εἰς ὑμᾶς.

3. τὸ μυστήριον. The secret revealed to him is that stated in verse 6.

καθὼς προέγραψα ἐν ὀλίγῳ. It is generally supposed that the writing here mentioned is to be found in the first chapter of this Epistle (especially in i. 9—14); but may it not refer to a previous letter? The hypothesis of such a letter having been written not long before would help to explain the absence of personal and other special details in this letter.

4. πρὸς ὅ, "by reference to which," namely, what I wrote.

ἀναγινώσκοντες νοῆσαι τὴν σύνεσίν μου ἐν τῷ μυσ-
5 τηρίῳ τοῦ Χριστοῦ, ὃ ἑτέραις γενεαῖς οὐκ ἐγνωρίσθη
τοῖς υἱοῖς τῶν ἀνθρώπων ὡς νῦν ἀπεκαλύφθη τοῖς
ἁγίοις ἀποστόλοις αὐτοῦ καὶ προφήταις ἐν πνεύματι,
6 εἶναι τὰ ἔθνη συγκληρονόμα καὶ σύσσωμα καὶ συμ-
μέτοχα τῆς ἐπαγγελίας ἐν Χριστῷ Ἰησοῦ διὰ τοῦ
7 εὐαγγελίου, οὗ ἐγενήθην διάκονος κατὰ τὴν δωρεὰν
τῆς χάριτος τοῦ θεοῦ τὴν δοθεῖσάν μοι κατὰ τὴν
8 ἐνέργειαν τῆς δυνάμεως αὐτοῦ. ἐμοὶ τῷ ἐλαχισ-
τοτέρῳ πάντων ἁγίων ἐδόθη ἡ χάρις αὕτη, ἐν τοῖς
ἔθνεσιν εὐαγγελίσασθαι τὸ ἀνεξιχνίαστον πλοῦτος
9 τοῦ Χριστοῦ, καὶ φωτίσαι πάντας τίς ἡ οἰκονομία
τοῦ μυστηρίου τοῦ ἀποκεκρυμμένου ἀπὸ τῶν αἰώνων
10 ἐν τῷ θεῷ τῷ τὰ πάντα κτίσαντι, ἵνα γνωρισθῇ νῦν
ταῖς ἀρχαῖς καὶ ταῖς ἐξουσίαις ἐν τοῖς ἐπουρανίοις
διὰ τῆς ἐκκλησίας ἡ πολυποίκιλος σοφία τοῦ θεοῦ,
11 κατὰ πρόθεσιν τῶν αἰώνων ἣν ἐποίησεν ἐν Χριστῷ
12 Ἰησοῦ τῷ κυρίῳ ἡμῶν, ἐν ᾧ ἔχομεν τὴν παρρησίαν

6. That the Gentiles should be associated with the Jews in all their privileges and expectations.

9. φωτίσαι πάντας τίς ἡ οἰκονομία τοῦ μυστηρίου. The enlightening is the same as that spoken of in 2 Cor. iv. 4, 6. εἰς τὸ μὴ αὐγάσαι τὸν φωτισμὸν τοῦ εὐαγγελίου τῆς δόξης τοῦ Χριστοῦ. πρὸς φωτισμὸν τῆς γνώσεως τῆς δόξης τοῦ θεοῦ ἐν προσώπῳ Ἰησοῦ Χριστοῦ. It seems doubtful whether οἰκονομία here is to be taken as in this chapter, verse 2, or as in i. 10. In the former case, "the dispensation of the mystery" would mean the distribution of it, the giving it out to men. Compare οἰκονόμους μυστηρίων θεοῦ, 1 Cor. iv. 1. In the latter, "the dispensation of the mystery" would be the system or Divine economy introduced by the unfolding of God's hidden purpose. Perhaps this latter sense suits the context best.

10. ταῖς ἀρχαῖς καὶ ταῖς ἐξουσίαις ἐν τοῖς ἐπουρανίοις, the frequent expression in these two Epistles for the powers of the invisible world. Here no distinction of good or bad is implied; but an intellectual personality is ascribed to them.

12. τὴν παρρησίαν καὶ τὴν προσ-

καὶ τὴν προσαγωγὴν ἐν πεποιθήσει διὰ τῆς πίστεως
αὐτοῦ.
13 Διὸ αἰτοῦμαι μὴ ἐγκακεῖν ἐν ταῖς θλίψεσίν μου
14 ὑπὲρ ὑμῶν, ἥτις ἐστὶν δόξα ὑμῶν. τούτου χάριν
15 κάμπτω τὰ γόνατά μου πρὸς τὸν πατέρα, ἐξ οὗ πᾶσα
16 πατριὰ ἐν οὐρανοῖς καὶ ἐπὶ γῆς ὀνομάζεται, ἵνα δῴη
ὑμῖν κατὰ τὸ πλοῦτος τῆς δόξης αὐτοῦ δυνάμει κρα-
ταιωθῆναι διὰ τοῦ πνεύματος αὐτοῦ εἰς τὸν ἔσω
17 ἄνθρωπον, κατοικῆσαι τὸν Χριστὸν διὰ τῆς πίστεως
18 ἐν ταῖς καρδίαις ὑμῶν, ἐν ἀγάπῃ ἐῤῥιζωμένοι καὶ

αγωγήν. Compare ii. 18; Heb. x. 19.

13. Compare the striking words in Col. i. 24. "Tribulations" were necessary for the building up of the Church. By this use they were made sacred, and might be a source of rejoicing to him who suffered and to them for whom they were endured.

14. The sentence, interrupted after verse 1, is now taken up and proceeds. The omission of the words τοῦ Κυρίου ἡμῶν Ἰησοῦ Χριστοῦ after τὸν πατέρα, on undoubted MS. authority, should be observed. The Vulgate, whilst retaining these words, exhibited the connexion of the next clause with τὸν πατέρα by rendering πᾶσα πατριά omnis paternitas.

15. πατριά is evidently used with reference to the preceding πατήρ. The *Name* of the Father, according to Scriptural conceptions, is real and vital; and to say that every πατριά is *named* after the Father means that the Fatherhood of God is the source and ground of every such association. Every family, every clan (πατριά), has its bond in a common father; and an earthly father is an image and representative of the heavenly. All family unions, all fellowships which acknowledge a πατήρ, are based upon the *Name of the one Father*.

It is not obvious why St. Paul introduced *here* this unfolding of what is contained in the Name of the Father. It is enough to say that it helps to make the whole grand image of the filial fellowship of men with God in the Son a more living one.

16. εἰς τὸν ἔσω ἄνθρωπον. Is this merely "in the inner man," in the inward spiritual nature? or is it "unto the inner man," so as to mature the true man, the image of God, the Christ in each man? In the latter case the "inner man" corresponds with the "new man" of iv. 24.

τεθεμελιωμένοι, ἵνα ἐξισχύσητε καταλαβέσθαι σὺν πᾶσιν τοῖς ἁγίοις τί τὸ πλάτος καὶ μῆκος καὶ βάθος
19 καὶ ὕψος, γνῶναί τε τὴν ὑπερβάλλουσαν τῆς γνώσεως ἀγάπην τοῦ Χριστοῦ, ἵνα πληρωθῆτε εἰς πᾶν τὸ πλήρωμα τοῦ θεοῦ.
20 Τῷ δὲ δυναμένῳ ὑπὲρ πάντα ποιῆσαι ὑπερεκπερισσοῦ ὧν αἰτούμεθα ἢ νοοῦμεν κατὰ τὴν δύναμιν
21 τὴν ἐνεργουμένην ἐν ἡμῖν, αὐτῷ ἡ δόξα ἐν τῇ ἐκκλησίᾳ ἐν Χριστῷ Ἰησοῦ εἰς πάσας τὰς γενεὰς τοῦ αἰῶνος τῶν αἰώνων· ἀμήν.

18. ἐξισχύσητε, "may have strength to ..." Spiritual force and stability, a root and foundation of love, are necessary to enable the weak heart of a man to enter into the infinity of the Divine Love.

τί τὸ πλάτος, κ.τ.λ., "the breadth, and length, and depth, and height," —of what? If any definite word is understood, it must be Love, the Love of Christ. But it is possible that St. Paul did not intend anything definite to be understood, but referred generally to the Divine nature and purposes. "That you may know what is the breadth, and length, and depth, and height,"—of the Immeasurable.

19. "The love of Christ," *i.e.* Christ's love, which transcends knowledge, which no human knowledge can compass. A genitive after ὑπερβάλλειν, though rare, is not without precedent.

εἰς πᾶν τὸ πλήρωμα τοῦ θεοῦ, "unto (or up to) all God's fulness;" that ye may be filled to the perfect fulness,—that which is according to God's design.

20. κατὰ τὴν δύναμιν τὴν ἐνεργουμένην ἐν ἡμῖν. It is to be noticed how repeatedly St. Paul connects the most supreme operations of God's power with his operations *in us*. The power of God is *one*,—an essentially vital, restorative, and fatherly power. That which wrought in raising Christ up from the dead is the same which works in quickening the humblest soul.

21. The terms used here to express an indefinite duration may be thus explained. Time was conceived of as a succession of ages, αἰῶνες. An age of ages was a greater cycle comprising many lesser cycles. "Unto all the generations of the age of ages."

1 Παρακαλῶ οὖν ὑμᾶς ἐγὼ ὁ δέσμιος ἐν κυρίῳ, ἀξίως
2 περιπατῆσαι τῆς κλήσεως ἧς ἐκλήθητε, μετὰ πάσης
ταπεινοφροσύνης καὶ πραΰτητος, μετὰ μακροθυμίας,
3 ἀνεχόμενοι ἀλλήλων ἐν ἀγάπῃ, σπουδάζοντες τηρεῖν
τὴν ἑνότητα τοῦ πνεύματος ἐν τῷ συνδέσμῳ τῆς
4 εἰρήνης. ἓν σῶμα καὶ ἓν πνεῦμα, καθὼς καὶ ἐκλήθητε
5 ἐν μιᾷ ἐλπίδι τῆς κλήσεως ὑμῶν· εἷς κύριος, μία
6 πίστις, ἓν βάπτισμα· εἷς θεὸς καὶ πατὴρ πάντων,
7 ὁ ἐπὶ πάντων καὶ διὰ πάντων καὶ ἐν πᾶσιν. ἑνὶ δὲ
ἑκάστῳ ἡμῶν ἐδόθη ἡ χάρις κατὰ τὸ μέτρον τῆς

IV. 1. See the Introduction, p. 24.

2. ἀνεχόμενοι ἀλλήλων, "enduring at one another's hands." Compare "Ἕως πότε ἀνέξομαι ὑμῶν; St. Matt. xvii. 17.

3. τηρεῖν, "to keep by giving heed to..." ἐν τῷ συνδέσμῳ τῆς εἰρήνης. ἐν is "within." Peace is regarded as a bond holding all in harmony together where the unity of the Spirit is heeded. In Col. iii. 14, love is called "the bond of perfectness" in a similar sense.

4. Ἓν σῶμα. On the whole the ordinary punctuation seems to be the best. "There is one body,..."

καθὼς καὶ ἐκλήθητε ἐν μιᾷ ἐλπίδι. The calling was made by means of the holding forth of a hope. This hope was one and the same for all who received the Gospel. It was the hope of filial adoption or sonship. This being the nature of the calling, it was in harmony with it (καθὼς καὶ ἐκλήθητε) that there should be one body and one spirit for those who were called.

6. The first πάντων refers to those who are exhorted to unity: "you all have one God and Father." In the second clause the reference is more general, probably to all *things*, as well as all persons.

7. Unity is not incompatible with variety. Each member of the one body has his particular duties and gifts.

ἡ χάρις. Hardly "grace," in the sense of spiritual influence; but rather "his special grace or privilege." We have seen that St. Paul habitually regarded his own life-work as his χάρις (iii. 7). He might apply the same language to others. "Each one amongst us has had his grace given him," has been favoured with his own appointment, has had his office bestowed upon him. Compare Rom. xii. 6, ἔχοντες χαρίσματα κατὰ τὴν χάριν τὴν δοθεῖσαν ἡμῖν διάφορα.

8 δωρεᾶς τοῦ Χριστοῦ. διὸ λέγει Ἀναβὰς εἰς ὕψος ᾐχμαλώτευσεν αἰχμαλωσίαν, ἔδωκεν δόματα τοῖς ἀν-
9 θρώποις. τὸ δὲ ἀνέβη τί ἐστιν εἰ μὴ ὅτι καὶ κατέβη

8. διὸ λέγει, scil. ἡ γραφή. "It says," i.e. the Scripture. What follows is a free quotation of an originally obscure passage, Psalm lxviii. 18. If we say that St. Paul simply adduced words which struck upon his memory from the sacred books, for the sake of expressing more pointedly what he wanted to teach, and did not necessarily concern himself about the sense of the passage in the original nor about exact accuracy in quotation, we must bear in mind also that St. Paul was not really resting any conclusion upon the dogmatic authority of the passage he quotes. Here, for example, it would be absurd to suppose that he is *proving* the fact of the Divine distribution of offices and gifts by an appeal to the Hebrew Scriptures.

It is singular, however, that he should have altered the passage he quotes so much as he appears to have done. The Psalm speaks of the going up of the ark of Jehovah to the summit of Zion. The second clause of the verse quoted is thus given by the Septuagint, which is said to agree with the Hebrew original: ἔλαβες δόματα ἐν ἀνθρώποις, (or ἐν ἀνθρώπῳ,)—which is interpreted to mean, "thou hast received gifts in men," that is, "thou hast received men as gifts." This is very different from "thou hast *given* gifts *to* men;" and we do not know whether to attribute the variation to a mistake of memory, to extreme freedom in using resemblances of sound rather than of meaning, or to a feeling that in the change made he is *developing* the meaning of the original words. This passage reminds us of what St. Peter said (Acts ii. 33), "Being therefore exalted by the right hand of God and *having received* from the Father the promise of the Holy Ghost, *he has shed forth* this which you see and hear." It is just possible that St. Paul's thoughts ran thus: "When he ascended up on high he took a multitude of captives, and received gifts in men, and then gave the gifts (namely, human offices) which he had received," and that he omitted, as not necessary for his purpose, the middle part of the sentence. But neither this, nor any other explanation which has been suggested, can be said to be satisfactory.

9. τὸ δὲ ἀνέβη. "But when we say that he ascended, what is implied but that he also descended first to the lower parts of the earth?" There is little to enable us to decide whether by "the

10 εἰς τὰ κατώτερα τῆς γῆς; ὁ καταβὰς αὐτός ἐστιν καὶ
ὁ ἀναβὰς ὑπεράνω πάντων τῶν οὐρανῶν, ἵνα πληρώσῃ
11 τὰ πάντα. καὶ αὐτὸς ἔδωκεν τοὺς μὲν ἀποστόλους,
τοὺς δὲ προφήτας, τοὺς δὲ εὐαγγελιστάς, τοὺς δὲ
12 ποιμένας καὶ διδασκάλους, πρὸς τὸν καταρτισμὸν τῶν

lower parts of the earth" we are to understand parts below the surface of the earth, or simply the parts of this earth, which are low down in relation to the heaven above.

Why should St. Paul insist here upon the identification of him who went up with him who came down?—In order, it would seem, to bring to his readers' minds the recollection of the historical Jesus who had died and been raised again.

11. καὶ αὐτὸς ἔδωκεν. "And he it is who has given." Then follow examples of various χάριτες given to members of the one body. We are not to suppose that each of the functions here named had a formal office answering to it in the Christian Church. Compare 1 Cor. xii. 28. The title ἀπόστολος itself was not always confined to the Twelve and St. Paul. See 2 Cor. viii. 23; Phil. ii. 25.

προφήτας. Expounders, declaring the will of God with authority. See especially 1 Cor. xiv. The recognised προφῆται were accustomed also to deliver predictions. Acts xii. 27, 28; xxi. 10, 11.

εὐαγγελιστάς, persons employed in proclaiming the glad tidings. Philip, one of the Seven, is called (Acts xxi. 8) an evangelist, as if this title described a distinct office; but, on the other hand, Timothy is charged (2 Tim. iv. 5) to "do the work of an evangelist."

ποιμένας καὶ διδασκάλους. The term *shepherd* implies the functions of *ruling*, almost more than that of supplying spiritual food. Here, the same persons are represented as doing the work both of shepherds and teachers.

12. πρὸς τὸν καταρτισμὸν τῶν ἁγίων, "for the organizing of the saints, unto the work of ministering, unto the building of the body of Christ." The clause εἰς ἔργον διακονίας, without being strictly governed in one sentence by καταρτισμόν (with the meaning, "to qualify the saints for the work of ministering") may be rather dependent on, than in apposition with, the preceding clause. The organizing of the Church is the purpose of the functions just described, and the result of this organization is practical activity in ministering, and a building up of the body of Christ.

τὸν κατ. τῶν ἁγίων *might* mean

ἁγίων εἰς ἔργον διακονίας, εἰς οἰκοδομὴν τοῦ σώματος
13 τοῦ Χριστοῦ, μέχρι καταντήσωμεν οἱ πάντες εἰς τὴν
ἑνότητα τῆς πίστεως καὶ τῆς ἐπιγνώσεως τοῦ υἱοῦ τοῦ
θεοῦ, εἰς ἄνδρα τέλειον, εἰς μέτρον ἡλικίας τοῦ πλη-
14 ρώματος τοῦ Χριστοῦ, ἵνα μηκέτι ὦμεν νήπιοι, κλυδωνι-
ζόμενοι καὶ περιφερόμενοι παντὶ ἀνέμῳ τῆς διδασκαλίας
ἐν τῇ κυβείᾳ τῶν ἀνθρώπων, ἐν πανουργίᾳ πρὸς τὴν
15 μεθοδείαν τῆς πλάνης, ἀληθεύοντες δὲ ἐν ἀγάπῃ

the perfecting of individual character, but it seems most suitable to the general use of καταρτίζω and to the context to take τῶν ἁγίων as the aggregate of believers, and the work upon them as that of adjusting them in their mutual relations to one another.

13. "Until we all (arrive at) attain to the unity of the faith and of the knowledge of the Son of God."

οἱ πάντες. Observe the article. St. Paul is throughout speaking of the members of the Church as forming a body, and not as individuals. "Until the whole body arrives at..."

τὴν ἑνότητα, the unity which depends on believing in and knowing the Son of God.

εἰς ἄνδρα τέλειον. "Unto a full-grown Man." The Man is the body of believers.

εἰς μέτρον ἡλικίας. The image is carried on. "Unto the measure of growth of the fulness of Christ." ἡλικία is age, or time of life; and by an easy transition it represents a stage of growth or maturity.

"The fulness of Christ" stands for the perfection of Humanity, the stage when Christ is complete in his body and all its members.

14. Placing a comma after πανουργίᾳ, and none after διδασκαλίας or ἀνθρώπων, we may translate, "carried about by every wind of teaching in the craft of men in knavery;"—the changes of teaching having the craft of men for their element, and that craft having knavery for *its* element.

πρὸς τὴν μεθοδείαν τῆς πλάνης, "to the following out of error." This seems to be the meaning of the rare word μεθοδεία. μεθοδεύω is "to pursue, to track, to treat a subject by rule or method;" and so comes to mean "to pursue by craft, to outwit:" but this latter sense hardly suits the present passage. St. Paul refers to the effect of such teaching as he describes, in methodical and systematic false doctrine.

15. ἀληθεύοντες, not *speaking* the truth, merely, but "observing, or being loyal to, truth," in con-

αὐξήσωμεν εἰς αὐτὸν τὰ πάντα, ὅς ἐστιν ἡ κεφαλή, 16 Χριστός, ἐξ οὗ πᾶν τὸ σῶμα συναρμολογούμενον καὶ συμβιβαζόμενον διὰ πάσης ἁφῆς τῆς ἐπιχορηγίας κατ᾽ ἐνέργειαν ἐν μέτρῳ ἑνὸς ἑκάστου μέρους τὴν αὔξησιν τοῦ σώματος ποιεῖται εἰς οἰκοδομὴν ἑαυτοῦ ἐν ἀγάπῃ.

17 Τοῦτο οὖν λέγω καὶ μαρτύρομαι ἐν κυρίῳ, μηκέτι ὑμᾶς περιπατεῖν καθὼς καὶ τὰ λοιπὰ ἔθνη περιπατεῖ 18 ἐν ματαιότητι τοῦ νοὸς αὐτῶν, ἐσκοτισμένοι τῇ διανοίᾳ ὄντες, ἀπηλλοτριωμένοι τῆς ζωῆς τοῦ θεοῦ, διὰ τὴν

trast with the indifference to truth just described.

ἐν ἀγάπῃ may be said to belong to both ἀληθεύοντες and αὐξήσωμεν, rather than to either exclusively: "but being loyal to truth may in love grow up..."

16. See the translation. The terms in this description of the growth of the body are crowded together, as is not uncommon in St. Paul, and in the end the sentence states that "the body... effects the growth of the body." But the sense of the passage is plain enough. The aim of the Apostle is to express the vital action of every part in its place, and at the same time the dependence of all the parts on the head.

ἐξ οὗ, from whom, depending on whom. διὰ πάσης ἁφῆς τῆς ἐπιχορηγίας.

There is some doubt as to the meaning of the word ἐπιχορηγία in this clause. We cannot render, as in E. V., "the supply of every joint." We must keep the order of the words and read, "by means of every joint (or ligature) of the supply;" nearly equivalent to "every joining supplied," "the supply" being the whole amount or material supplied. The ἁφαί of the body of Christ are the *relations* of the members one to another.

κατ᾽ ἐνέργειαν, as well as ἐν μέτρῳ, goes with ἑνὸς ἑκάστου μέρους.

18. τῆς ζωῆς τοῦ θεοῦ. St. Paul has spoken before in this Epistle, as elsewhere, of that quickening power with which God raises and renews the soul. Compare, in the way of contrast, i. 18—ii. 5; the enlightenment and knowledge there spoken of with the darkness and ignorance here; the life, shared with Christ, with the estrangement from that life.

With this description of the state of the Gentile world, compare that in Romans i. 21 to the end. The elements of the description, and many of the terms, are

ἄγνοιαν τὴν οὖσαν ἐν αὐτοῖς, διὰ τὴν πώρωσιν τῆς
19 καρδίας αὐτῶν, οἵτινες ἀπηλγηκότες ἑαυτοὺς παρέδωκαν
τῇ ἀσελγείᾳ εἰς ἐργασίαν ἀκαθαρσίας πάσης ἐν πλεο-
20 νεξίᾳ. ὑμεῖς δὲ οὐχ οὕτως ἐμάθετε τὸν Χριστόν,
21 εἴ γε αὐτὸν ἠκούσατε καὶ ἐν αὐτῷ ἐδιδάχθητε καθὼς
22 ἐστιν ἀλήθεια ἐν τῷ Ἰησοῦ, ἀποθέσθαι ὑμᾶς κατὰ
τὴν προτέραν ἀναστροφὴν τὸν παλαιὸν ἄνθρωπον τὸν
23 φθειρόμενον κατὰ τὰς ἐπιθυμίας τῆς ἀπάτης, ἀνανε-
24 οῦσθαι δὲ τῷ πνεύματι τοῦ νοὸς ὑμῶν καὶ ἐνδύσασθαι

the same in both passages. The emptiness, the darkness, the ignorance, the callousness, the ungoverned sensuality, which characterised the Gentile mind, are in both places set forth.

20. οὐχ οὕτως, "not so," not that you should be or remain in such a state.

ἐμάθετε τὸν Χριστόν. *Christ himself* was the object of learning and study to the believers; his nature, his character, his work and power, the purpose of God manifested in him. Compare Hebrews iii. 1. κατανοήσατε τὸν ἀπόστολον καὶ ἀρχιερέα τῆς ὁμολογίας ἡμῶν Ἰησοῦν.

21. εἴ γε αὐτὸν ἠκούσατε, "if you have heard him," his voice calling you.

ἐν αὐτῷ, certainly not "*by* him" as in E. V., but "in him," either with the usual sense of ἐν κυρίῳ or ἐν Χριστῷ, when this expression is used to denote the whole state or conditions of being of the Christian,—or with the more special meaning, that Christ is the subject or element of knowledge. This latter meaning appears the most suitable to the passage, especially when we take into consideration the words immediately following.

καθώς ἐστιν ἀλήθεια ἐν τῷ Ἰησοῦ, "as truth is, or as there is truth, in Jesus." Truth is the matter of the teaching. "If you have learnt that truth which is to be found in Jesus." Λέγει αὐτῷ ὁ Ἰησοῦς, Ἐγώ εἰμι ἡ ὁδὸς καὶ ἡ ἀλήθεια. (St. John xiv. 6.)

22. ἀποθέσθαι, "namely, that you should put off..." This was the purport of what they had been taught.

τὸν φθειρόμενον. Observe the tense. "Which is being corrupted, or brought to destruction." κατὰ τὰς ἐπ-, "according to," under the influence of... τὰς ἐπιθυμίας τῆς ἀπάτης, the lusts which are the instruments or servants of deceit.

24. The "new man" is the ideal existing in God's mind. As such, it is already "created."

τὸν καινὸν ἄνθρωπον τὸν κατὰ θεὸν κτισθέντα ἐν δικαιοσύνῃ καὶ ὁσιότητι τῆς ἀληθείας. 25 Διὸ ἀποθέμενοι τὸ ψεῦδος λαλεῖτε ἀλήθειαν ἕκαστος μετὰ τοῦ πλησίον αὐτοῦ, ὅτι ἐσμὲν ἀλλήλων μέλη. 26 ὀργίζεσθε καὶ μὴ ἁμαρτάνετε· ὁ ἥλιος μὴ ἐπιδυέτω 27 ἐπὶ τῷ παροργισμῷ ὑμῶν, μηδὲ δίδοτε τόπον τῷ 28 διαβόλῳ. ὁ κλέπτων μηκέτι κλεπτέτω, μᾶλλον δὲ κοπιάτω ἐργαζόμενος τὸ ἀγαθὸν ταῖς χερσίν, ἵνα ἔχῃ 29 μεταδιδόναι τῷ χρείαν ἔχοντι. πᾶς λόγος σαπρὸς ἐκ τοῦ στόματος ὑμῶν μὴ ἐκπορευέσθω, ἀλλ' εἴ τις ἀγαθὸς πρὸς οἰκοδομὴν τῆς χρείας, ἵνα δῷ χάριν τοῖς 30 ἀκούουσιν. καὶ μὴ λυπεῖτε τὸ πνεῦμα τὸ ἅγιον τοῦ θεοῦ, ἐν ᾧ ἐσφραγίσθητε εἰς ἡμέραν ἀπολυτρώσεως.

κατὰ θεόν is not quite "in the likeness of God." It means "in accordance with God's will and nature." "The righteousness and holiness of truth" answer to "the lusts of deceit." Truth is represented as a power presiding over righteousness and holiness.

26. ὀργίζεσθε καὶ μὴ ἁμαρτάνετε. Quoted from Ps. iv. 5 (or 4) Sept. Anger or resentment is not necessarily and intrinsically evil, but it ought not to be cherished, so as to become enmity. "If you are made angry by anything, let not your irritation last over the day."

27. τῷ διαβόλῳ. Διάβολος = ὃς διαβάλλει, the evil spirit which sets man against man and man against God. Luther's Version has "dem Lästerer," "to the slanderer," probably meaning the human slanderer. In translating διάβολος by "the devil," the moral significance of the term ought never to be lost sight of, as it is never neglected when the word is used in the New Testament. In the present case St. Paul implies that the cherishing of anger would be giving room for the spirit of misunderstanding and enmity to come in.

29. σαπρός, literally "decayed or rotten." πρὸς οἰκοδομὴν τῆς χρείας, "for edification suggested by the need, or the occasion."

ἵνα δῷ χάριν. After δῷ, χάρις can hardly be taken in the general sense of Grace. "That it may give a grace," or impart a benefit.

30. Corrupting communications are an especial outrage upon the Spirit which makes the Church holy.

ἐν ᾧ ἐσφραγίσθητε. See the note

31 πᾶσα πικρία καὶ θυμὸς καὶ ὀργὴ καὶ
32 βλασφημία ἀρθήτω ἀφ' ὑμῶν σὺν πάσῃ κακίᾳ. γίνεσθε δὲ εἰς ἀλλήλους χρηστοί, εὔσπλαγχνοι, χαριζόμενοι ἑαυτοῖς καθὼς καὶ ὁ θεὸς ἐν Χριστῷ ἐχαρίσατο ὑμῖν.

V. 1 Γίνεσθε οὖν μιμηταὶ τοῦ θεοῦ, ὡς τέκνα ἀγαπητά,
2 καὶ περιπατεῖτε ἐν ἀγάπῃ, καθὼς καὶ ὁ Χριστὸς ἠγάπησεν ὑμᾶς καὶ παρέδωκεν ἑαυτὸν ὑπὲρ ὑμῶν προσφορὰν καὶ θυσίαν τῷ θεῷ εἰς ὀσμὴν εὐωδίας.
3 Πορνεία δὲ καὶ ἀκαθαρσία πᾶσα ἢ πλεονεξία μηδὲ
4 ὀνομαζέσθω ἐν ὑμῖν, καθὼς πρέπει ἁγίοις, καὶ αἰσχρότης καὶ μωρολογία ἢ εὐτραπελία, τὰ οὐκ ἀνήκοντα,
5 ἀλλὰ μᾶλλον εὐχαριστία. τοῦτο γὰρ ἴστε γινώ-

on i. 13, and compare again 2 Cor. i. 22, "who has also sealed us and given us the earnest of the Spirit in our hearts."

32. St. Paul urges the Gospel doctrine, that God's forgiveness, if truly received, must work in us forgiveness towards our brother.

V. 1. ὡς τέκνα. It is the nature of a child to imitate his father.

2. παρέδωκεν, "gave himself up," not exactly in the sense of "presenting," but rather of "surrendering." The idea of presentation to God is contained in the following words προσφορὰν καὶ θυσίαν τῷ θεῷ. Of these terms it may be said that, although they are frequently used as synonymous, θυσία is a more special term than προσφορά and denotes a sacrifice slain and burnt on the altar. It was an ancient and wide-spread piece of symbolism, to regard the smoke of the burning victim as sweet to the nostrils of the divinity to whom it was offered (Gen. viii. 21, &c.). Here the self-surrender of the Son of God is represented as most pleasing to the Father, in accordance with whose will it was made. In Philip. iv. 18, the Apostle calls the gift sent him from Philippi, ὀσμὴν εὐωδίας, θυσίαν δεκτήν, εὐάρεστον τῷ θεῷ, where the sweet smell appears to refer, in part at least, to himself.

5. τοῦτο γὰρ ἴστε γινώσκοντες. It is not easy to explain why this peculiar form of expression should have been used here. "This you are aware of, knowing it," or "This you know and are aware of." The reading of the received text, ἐστέ, would not be easier.

σκοντες ὅτι πᾶς πόρνος ἢ ἀκάθαρτος ἢ πλεονέκτης, ὅς ἐστιν εἰδωλολάτρης, οὐκ ἔχει κληρονομίαν ἐν τῇ
6 βασιλείᾳ τοῦ Χριστοῦ καὶ θεοῦ. μηδεὶς ὑμᾶς ἀπατάτω κενοῖς λόγοις· διὰ ταῦτα γὰρ ἔρχεται ἡ ὀργὴ τοῦ
7 θεοῦ ἐπὶ τοὺς υἱοὺς τῆς ἀπειθείας. μὴ οὖν γίνεσθε
8 συμμέτοχοι αὐτῶν. ἦτε γάρ ποτε σκότος, νῦν δὲ

πλεονέκτης, ὅς ἐστιν εἰδωλολάτρης. So in Col. iii. 5. Compare Job xxxi. 24, "If I have made gold my hope, or have said to the fine gold, Thou art my confidence...;" 1 Tim. vi. 17.

6. κενοῖς λόγοις,—as if God were not caring for men's sins, or as if these sins were necessary elements in human life. God is really angry on account of them; and the calamities of the world, both ordinary and extraordinary, are his judgments to punish men for them.

8—14. This should be studied as a great passage concerning Light, in its spiritual sense. It is vigorously conceived and expressed, like one of the thoughts which has been most thoroughly matured in St. Paul's mind.

"You were once *darkness*,"—not merely *darkened*, as above, or *in* darkness. Similarly he says, in 2 Cor. v. 21, that God has made Christ *sin*, that we might be made *righteousness*. St. Paul means to express *more* by such language than the ordinary mode of speaking could have conveyed. Yet it is not a superlative degree of moral darkness or enlightenment which he seeks to describe. As it is so often necessary to remind ourselves, St. Paul is not thinking of the stage to which the individual character had fallen or risen, but of *the condition* to which the individual character was subject and obedient. That condition was, in the old case, Darkness; in the new case, Light. And in his present affirmations, St. Paul is expressing his sense of the law by which the condition,—the Light or the Darkness,—*appropriates and assimilates* the souls subject to it. Souls subject to the darkness become a part of the darkness: souls subject to the Light become a part of the Light.

There is therefore here a special significance in the phrase "children of light." You are adopted into Light; your new nature is the nature of Light; therefore walk as beings born anew in that nature. And *the exhortation* to "walk as children of light" is manifestly more in place after the expression of such an idea as that of the dominating and absorbing power of light, than if St. Paul

9 φῶς ἐν κυρίῳ· ὡς τέκνα φωτὸς περιπατεῖτε, ὁ γὰρ
καρπὸς τοῦ φωτὸς ἐν πάσῃ ἀγαθωσύνῃ καὶ δικαιοσύνῃ
10 καὶ ἀληθείᾳ, δοκιμάζοντες τί ἐστιν εὐάρεστον τῷ
11 κυρίῳ, καὶ μὴ συγκοινωνεῖτε τοῖς ἔργοις τοῖς ἀκάρποις
12 τοῦ σκότους, μᾶλλον δὲ καὶ ἐλέγχετε. τὰ γὰρ κρυφῆ
13 γινόμενα ὑπ' αὐτῶν αἰσχρόν ἐστιν καὶ λέγειν· τὰ δὲ
πάντα ἐλεγχόμενα ὑπὸ τοῦ φωτὸς φανεροῦται· πᾶν

had said, "You are all extremely enlightened persons." It would not have been inconsistent for him to say, "You are light in the Lord: why will you still love darkness and walk in it?"

9. "*The fruit of the light.*" The substitution of "the Spirit" for "light" is one of the most lamentable errors in our Received Version. It grievously spoils this noble passage.

10. The "proof" intended is that of trial and experience. The idea here expressed was a favourite one with St. Paul. Compare Rom. xii. 2, "that you may prove what is the will of God;" Phil. i. 10; 1 Thess. v. 21, 22. The children of light are not supplied with a complete literal directory of conduct, either in the Scriptures or in any other form. They must act in obedience to principle and according to their light, and so they will *find out*, by means of mistakes as well as of success, what God's will is.

11. The works of light are *fruit:* the works of darkness are *barren*. Compare Rom. vi. 21, 22, "What fruit had you then...? but now you have your fruit unto holiness."

μᾶλλον δὲ καὶ ἐλέγχετε. "But rather even (καὶ) *convict* them." Be not content with not having fellowship with them: so bring your light to bear upon them as to expose and convict them. Reproof, spoken reproof, might come in as *a part of* this work of convicting: but the whole effect of a life of light upon deeds of darkness seems to be in the Apostle's mind. The idea agrees exactly with that of St. John iii. 20, 21, "Every one that doeth evil hateth the light, and cometh not to the light, lest his deeds should be reproved (ἐλεγχθῇ): but he that doeth truth cometh to the light, that his deeds may be made manifest, that they are wrought in God."

13. It is a grammatical error in the Received Version to translate ἐλεγχόμενα as if it were τὰ ἐλεγχόμενα. But it makes little difference in the sense. ὑπὸ τοῦ φωτός probably goes with φανεροῦται, and the common derivation of φῶς and φανερός (φα·) is evidently

14 γὰρ τὸ φανερούμενον φῶς ἐστίν. διὸ λέγει Ἔγειρε ὁ καθεύδων καὶ ἀνάστα ἐκ τῶν νεκρῶν, καὶ ἐπιφαύσει σοι ὁ Χριστός.
15 Βλέπετε οὖν πῶς ἀκριβῶς περιπατεῖτε, μὴ ὡς ἄσοφοι
16 ἀλλ' ὡς σοφοί, ἐξαγοραζόμενοι τὸν καιρόν, ὅτι αἱ

brought into view. "But all deeds, when convicted, are made manifest by light; for all that is made manifest is light." It cannot be doubted that φανερούμενον is passive. As regards the sense of this verse, we must remember the first words of the passage, "You *are* now *light* in the Lord." It is physically true that whatever is brought out into a blaze of light becomes itself by reflection a source of light. And, in the sphere of moral or spiritual action, there is a remarkable affinity between the openness of broad daylight and purity or innocence. Dark deeds are done in secret (κρυφῇ): drag them into the light, and they cannot stand it. Thus a debased soul brought into open daylight, and not rushing from it, is naturally purified; that which was darkness, whilst in the dark, becomes light in the daylight. There is something of this feeling expressed in two sayings of Luther's: "I have often need, in my tribulations, to talk even with a child, in order to expel such thoughts as the devil possesses me with." "When I am assailed with heavy tribulations, I rush out among my pigs, rather than remain alone by myself." *Shame* is one of the influences by which the light conquers a soul from darkness.

14. A good example of the freedom with which St. Paul quotes from the Old Testament. His manner is entirely alien from that of one who is adducing a dogmatic proof: he is borrowing illustrative expressions, and has no sense of being debarred from modifying them to suit his purpose. The nearest words to these in St. Paul, introduced by "wherefore it says," *i.e.* the Scripture, are to be found in Isa. lx. 1, 2. His thought is that of the change from darkness to light,—a change produced by the opening of the eyes to the light shining in the face of Jesus Christ, he upon whom that light shines being thereby illuminated, and himself turned into light.

15. Literally, "Look therefore how you walk exactly, or accurately."

16. ἐξαγοραζόμενοι τὸν καιρόν, "buying up opportunity, or the right moment," like a merchant seeking some valuable but scarce

17 ἡμέραι πονηραί εἰσιν. διὰ τοῦτο μὴ γίνεσθε ἄφρονες,
18 ἀλλὰ συνιέντες τί τὸ θέλημα τοῦ κυρίου. καὶ μὴ μεθύσκεσθε οἴνῳ, ἐν ᾧ ἐστὶν ἀσωτία, ἀλλὰ πληροῦσθε
19 ἐν πνεύματι, λαλοῦντες ἑαυτοῖς ψαλμοῖς καὶ ὕμνοις καὶ ᾠδαῖς πνευματικαῖς, ᾄδοντες καὶ ψάλλοντες ἐν τῇ
20 καρδίᾳ ὑμῶν τῷ κυρίῳ, εὐχαριστοῦντες πάντοτε ὑπὲρ πάντων ἐν ὀνόματι τοῦ κυρίου ἡμῶν Ἰησοῦ Χριστοῦ
21 τῷ θεῷ καὶ πατρί, ὑποτασσόμενοι ἀλλήλοις ἐν φόβῳ

product. Amongst other points of prudence for those who would "walk warily in dangerous times" must be the observing of *the fit season* for each act. The following passage from Plato's Republic illustrates this idea: "Again, it is quite clear, I imagine, that if a person lets the right moment for any work go by, (ἐάν τίς τινος παρῇ ἔργου καιρόν,) it never returns. It is quite clear. For the thing to be done does not choose, I imagine, to tarry the leisure of the doer" (p. 370). But there is a sentence in Ecclesiasticus so similar to this of St. Paul's, that one could almost suppose that the echo of it was in his mind: Συντήρησον καιρὸν καὶ φύλαξαι ἀπὸ πονηροῦ (Ecclus. iv. 20). Perhaps its full force is to be given to ἐξαγοραζόμενοι, "buying out of, or away from," by regarding fit moments as won at the cost of some pains out of evil days.

18. πληροῦσθε ἐν πνεύματι. The contrast is between the "fulness" produced by wine, and another kind of fulness (also agreeable) produced by spiritual emotion. "Be filled—not with the intoxication of wine, but—in spirit." "Let the fulness you seek be spiritual fulness." We are naturally reminded of the remarks made on the Day of Pentecost (Acts ii. 13—16). It is clear that the Apostle was encouraging a state of mind marked by more than ordinary *excitement*. Meeting together and music and singing were to be the chief stimulants and indulgences of this excitement.

20, 21. What remarkable safeguards to such spiritual excitement are here subjoined!—Thanksgiving, intelligent and orderly, to the Father in the name of Christ; and mutual submission in the fear of God. No spiritual excitement, however highly wrought, could be injurious, that flowed between these banks.

ὑπὲρ πάντων. The preposition ὑπέρ might at first sight suggest that the thanks are to be given "on behalf of" all persons, especially as we find ἐπί used elsewhere to denote that for which

22 Χριστοῦ. Αἱ γυναῖκες τοῖς ἰδίοις ἀνδράσιν ὡς τῷ
23 κυρίῳ, ὅτι ἀνήρ ἐστιν κεφαλὴ τῆς γυναικὸς ὡς καὶ

thanks are given. But we have in 1 Cor. x. 30, τί βλασφημοῦμαι ὑπὲρ οὗ ἐγὼ εὐχαριστῶ; and it is better to keep the simpler meaning "for all things." The spiritual joy which was to have its root in thankfulness was also to be controlled by mutual respect and submission, experience having shewn (1 Cor. xiv.) the danger of rivalry and disorder amongst those who were yielding to spiritual excitement.

22. With Tischendorf's text, ὑποτάσσεσθε or ὑποτασσέσθωσαν must be *understood* from the preceding ὑποτασσόμενοι (verse 21). But many MSS. have one or the other of these words. Lachmann inserts the latter, and is supported by the Sinaitic MS.

ὡς τῷ κυρίῳ. It is obvious that the first apparent sense of this injunction,—that a wife should obey her husband without reserve as if he were the Lord,—cannot be the true one. St. Paul is not speaking of an individual case, but of the general law of married life. This law is based upon the facts, that the relation of husband and wife is Divinely ordained, and that it is an image of the relation between Christ and the Church. Now it is only in its ideal or perfect form that these statements can be absolutely true of the marriage-union; and St. Paul is speaking accordingly of the ideal husband and the ideal wife. The Christian wife is to discharge her duty to her husband as seeing the Lord, so to speak, in the background; the Christian husband is to discharge his to his wife as seeing the Church in the background. Such a law of conjugal duty is not made void by the imperfections attaching to actual married life. The wife of a bad husband has her submission often turned into opposition; she is often absolutely debarred from looking up to him. But still her feelings and her conduct will be affected by the presence in her mind of the ideal law of duty, which will struggle to assert itself so far as it is allowed. In the corresponding place in Col. we have the modified phrase ὡς ἀνῆκεν ἐν Κυρίῳ (iii. 18).

23. In both the volumes of Holy Scripture the relation of husband and wife frequently supplies the terms in which the union between the Divine Ruler and the human society is described. In the Old Testament, Jehovah is the husband, the race of Israel the wife. The unfaithfulness of the people of Israel to Jehovah is denounced as the sin of adultery. In Jer. iii. "backsliding Israel" and "her treacherous sister Judah" are *two* wives of Jehovah. Israel had been divorced on account of

ὁ Χριστὸς κεφαλὴ τῆς ἐκκλησίας, αὐτὸς σωτὴρ τοῦ
24 σώματος. ἀλλ᾽ ὡς ἡ ἐκκλησία ὑποτάσσεται τῷ
Χριστῷ, οὕτως καὶ αἱ γυναῖκες τοῖς ἀνδράσιν ἐν
25 παντί. Οἱ ἄνδρες, ἀγαπᾶτε τὰς γυναῖκας, καθὼς καὶ
ὁ Χριστὸς ἠγάπησεν τὴν ἐκκλησίαν καὶ ἑαυτὸν παρέ-
26 δωκεν ὑπὲρ αὐτῆς, ἵνα αὐτὴν ἁγιάσῃ καθαρίσας τῷ

her adulteries, and yet Judah feared not to be false also. Perhaps the most beautiful passage upon the union between Jehovah and the people of Israel is the prophetical outburst in Isa. liv. containing the words "For thy Maker is thine husband; the Lord of hosts is his name; and thy Redeemer, the Holy One of Israel; the God of the whole earth shall he be called" (verse 5). In the New Testament, the most striking presentations of this image are in the Apocalypse, where the Church, or the Heavenly Jerusalem, is spoken of as the Lamb's wife (Rev. xix. 7—9; xxi. 2, 3, 9, 10). What is peculiar to St. Paul here is the complication caused by the introduction of that other image, of a head and members, which he has made so specially his own.

αὐτὸς σωτὴρ τοῦ σώματος. The difficulty felt in understanding these words, together with the ἀλλά which follows, was early shewn by variations of reading. This clause appears to indicate a *difference* between the relation of Christ to the Church and that of the husband to the wife. "*He*," it is true, is more than the head, he is the "*Saviour* of the body"—with a play on σωτήρ and σώματος. This the husband has no pretensions to be: "nevertheless" (ἀλλά) let the *head*ship of the husband be acknowledged and acted upon.

24. ἐν παντί—not in certain departments of life, but universally or generally. Compare κατὰ πάντα, Col. iii. 20.

25—27. In translating this passage, we are placed at a disadvantage by having to choose between "her" and "it" for the rendering of the feminine pronoun. Neither is quite satisfactory. If we take "it," it is desirable to introduce into the passage some such word as "bride," to keep up the sense of the image.

There is a reference in these verses to the bath which it was the custom for the bride to take as one of the ceremonies preceding marriage. The Church was the Bride of Christ. What was her bath of purification?

The Church in every place was formed by the preaching of the Word. The Word was the message of forgiveness and reconciliation through Christ. Those who

27 λουτρῷ τοῦ ὕδατος ἐν ῥήματι, ἵνα παραστήσῃ αὐτὸς ἑαυτῷ ἔνδοξον τὴν ἐκκλησίαν, μὴ ἔχουσαν σπίλον ἢ ῥυτίδα ἤ τι τῶν τοιούτων, ἀλλ᾽ ἵνα ᾖ ἁγία καὶ ἄμωμος. 28 οὕτως καὶ οἱ ἄνδρες ὀφείλουσιν ἀγαπᾶν τὰς ἑαυτῶν γυναῖκας ὡς τὰ ἑαυτῶν σώματα. ὁ ἀγαπῶν τὴν ἑαυτοῦ 29 γυναῖκα ἑαυτὸν ἀγαπᾷ· οὐδεὶς γάρ ποτε τὴν ἑαυτοῦ σάρκα ἐμίσησεν, ἀλλὰ ἐκτρέφει καὶ θάλπει αὐτήν, 30 καθὼς καὶ ὁ Χριστὸς τὴν ἐκκλησίαν, ὅτι μέλη ἐσμὲν 31 τοῦ σώματος αὐτοῦ. ἀντὶ τούτου καταλείψει ἄνθρωπος πατέρα καὶ μητέρα καὶ προσκολληθήσεται πρὸς

received this message and yielded to the call, came out from the world, were baptized, and became members of a holy or consecrated community. Christ, then, gave himself up, in order that he might proclaim peace effectually to men and so might fashion for himself a pure Church.

It is the Word therefore (τὸ ῥῆμα, as in vi. 17), which is the great instrument of purification. And we are reminded of our Lord's words, St. John xv. 3 and xvii. 17: "You already are clean by reason of the word which I have spoken unto you;" "Sanctify them by thy truth: thy word is truth." The Word however had the ordinance of Baptism as its own instrument for effecting the separation of the Church from the world; and, although we might explain this passage without being compelled to introduce the baptismal washing, it is reasonable to suppose that in mentioning a laver or bath of water St. Paul had in his eye that actual external washing by means of which the Word symbolized and executed its work. It makes little difference whether we say that St. Paul was using the words τὸ λουτρὸν τοῦ ὕδατος himself in a figurative sense, or was naming that outward ceremony which was a visible figure for the same reality. The Lord's parting injunction to his Apostles included both the word and the outward washing. "Preach the Gospel, teach all nations; and baptize them in the Name of the Father, the Son, and the Holy Ghost."

27. αὐτὸς ἑαυτῷ. Emphasis is laid upon the fact that Christ is himself the doer of the whole work in the creation and cleansing of the Church.

30. The words ἐκ τῆς σαρκὸς αὐτοῦ καὶ ἐκ τῶν ὀστέων αὐτοῦ are added in good MSS. though not in the best. "We are members of his body, being made from his flesh and from his bones."

τὴν γυναῖκα αὐτοῦ, καὶ ἔσονται οἱ δύο εἰς σάρκα μίαν. τὸ μυστήριον τοῦτο μέγα ἐστίν, ἐγὼ δὲ λέγω εἰς Χριστὸν καὶ εἰς τὴν ἐκκλησίαν. πλὴν καὶ ὑμεῖς οἱ καθ' ἕνα ἕκαστος τὴν ἑαυτοῦ γυναῖκα οὕτως ἀγαπάτω ὡς ἑαυτόν, ἡ δὲ γυνὴ ἵνα φοβῆται τὸν ἄνδρα.

Τὰ τέκνα, ὑπακούετε τοῖς γονεῦσιν ὑμῶν ἐν κυρίῳ· τοῦτο γάρ ἐστιν δίκαιον. τίμα τὸν πατέρα σου καὶ τὴν μητέρα, ἥτις ἐστὶν ἐντολὴ πρώτη ἐν ἐπαγγελίᾳ, ἵνα εὖ σοι γένηται καὶ ἔσῃ μακροχρόνιος ἐπὶ τῆς γῆς. Καὶ οἱ πατέρες, μὴ παροργίζετε τὰ τέκνα ὑμῶν, ἀλλὰ ἐκτρέφετε αὐτὰ ἐν παιδείᾳ καὶ νουθεσίᾳ κυρίου.

Οἱ δοῦλοι, ὑπακούετε τοῖς κυρίοις κατὰ σάρκα μετὰ

31. Quoted literally from Gen. ii. 24, Sept. version.

32, 33. "*My* chief interest in this mystery" (ἐγώ is emphatic) "is as it relates to Christ and to the Church. But let all the married among you apply the mystery to their own case, so that the husband may love the wife and the wife fear the husband."

ἡ δὲ γυνὴ ἵνα φοβ. Supply, as in E. V. "Let the wife *see* that . . ."

VI. 1. ἐν κυρίῳ. Obey your parents, as an obligation of your Christian calling.

τοῦτο γάρ ἐστιν δίκαιον. By "righteous" St. Paul probably means here "in accordance with natural justice," or with the absolute laws and relations of human existence.

2. πρώτη. If the word "first" is understood as implying other commandments "with promise," they must be those which are not contained in the Decalogue. The "promise" refers rather to *national* than to individual prosperity and continuance.

4. μὴ παροργίζετε τὰ τέκνα, "do not try your children's tempers," especially by alternate indulgence and sharpness.

ἐν παιδείᾳ καὶ νουθεσίᾳ Κυρίου, "the discipline and instruction of the Lord," *i.e.* such as the Lord would approve, or such as befit those who belong to the Lord.

5. οἱ δοῦλοι, "bond-servants," slaves, not freemen serving for hire. There is considerable reiteration of the terms expressing servitude in this passage. The

φόβου καὶ τρόμου ἐν ἁπλότητι τῆς καρδίας ὑμῶν ὡς
6 τῷ Χριστῷ, μὴ κατ' ὀφθαλμοδουλείαν ὡς ἀνθρωπάρεσκοι ἀλλ' ὡς δοῦλοι Χριστοῦ ποιοῦντες τὸ
7 θέλημα τοῦ θεοῦ ἐκ ψυχῆς, μετ' εὐνοίας δουλεύοντες
8 ὡς τῷ κυρίῳ καὶ οὐκ ἀνθρώποις, εἰδότες ὅτι ὃ ἐάν
τι ἕκαστος ποιήσῃ ἀγαθόν, τοῦτο κομίσεται παρὰ
9 κυρίου, εἴτε δοῦλος εἴτε ἐλεύθερος. Καὶ οἱ κύριοι,
τὰ αὐτὰ ποιεῖτε πρὸς αὐτούς, ἀνιέντες τὴν ἀπειλήν,
εἰδότες ὅτι καὶ αὐτῶν καὶ ὑμῶν ὁ κύριός ἐστιν ἐν
οὐρανοῖς καὶ προσωπολημψία οὐκ ἔστιν παρ' αὐτῷ.
10 Τὸ λοιπόν, ἐνδυναμοῦσθε ἐν κυρίῳ καὶ ἐν τῷ
11 κράτει τῆς ἰσχύος αὐτοῦ. ἐνδύσασθε τὴν πανοπλίαν
τοῦ θεοῦ πρὸς τὸ δύνασθαι ὑμᾶς στῆναι πρὸς τὰς
12 μεθοδείας τοῦ διαβόλου, ὅτι οὐκ ἔστιν ἡμῖν ἡ πάλη

bond-servants were bond-servants, and must accept their condition. Their consolation and inward freedom were to be in the consciousness that they were serving Christ, when they loyally and cheerfully obeyed their masters: and *he* was a perfectly just master, whatever their masters according to the flesh might be.

9. τὰ αὐτὰ ποιεῖτε, "do the same things," act in the same conscientious and Christ-serving spirit.

προσωπολημψία, " respect or acceptance of *the person*" τοῦ προσώπου, that is, of the outside appearance, show, or profession, as distinguished from the inward reality. Compare Gal. ii. 6; 2 Cor. x. 1, 7.

10. This concluding passage, describing the Christian warfare, is not suggested by anything going before, but is evidently the free working-out of a familiar thought.

11. πρὸς τὰς μεθοδείας. As we might say, "*the tactics*" of the devil.

τοῦ διαβόλου. Let it be remembered that "the devil" (ὁ διαβάλλων) is the false accuser, the divider. In this passage his peculiar work, as setting men against God and against one another, is by no means to be left out of sight.

12. ἡ πάλη. The struggle is not so much that of the individual Christian, seeking his own salvation; but that of Christians united in a body and "striving together for the faith of the Gospel" (Phil. i. 27). The Church is

πρὸς αἷμα καὶ σάρκα, ἀλλὰ πρὸς τὰς ἀρχάς, πρὸς τὰς ἐξουσίας, πρὸς τοὺς κοσμοκράτορας τοῦ σκότους τούτου, πρὸς τὰ πνευματικὰ τῆς πονηρίας ἐν τοῖς 13 ἐπουρανίοις. διὰ τοῦτο ἀναλάβετε τὴν πανοπλίαν τοῦ θεοῦ, ἵνα δυνηθῆτε ἀντιστῆναι ἐν τῇ ἡμέρᾳ τῇ 14 πονηρᾷ καὶ ἅπαντα κατεργασάμενοι στῆναι. στῆτε οὖν περιζωσάμενοι τὴν ὀσφὺν ὑμῶν ἐν ἀληθείᾳ, καὶ

brought into conflict with spiritual enemies, the powers of darkness, by its task of spreading and establishing the kingdom of Light.

πρὸς αἷμα καὶ σάρκα. The Church was tempted to regard hostile *men* as its ultimate enemies; but behind these, and using external human agencies as their instruments, were invisible powers of evil.

ἀρχάς, ἐξουσίας, i. 21; iii. 10; Col. i. 16; ii. 10, 15. Compare Rom. viii. 38, οὔτε ἄγγελοι οὔτε ἀρχαὶ οὔτε δυνάμεις. Generally these terms are used in a neutral sense, not connoting either goodness or badness. The vagueness of such terms, so far as questions of nature and personality are concerned, appears to be intentional on St. Paul's part. It is quite probable that he meant by "principalities and powers" distinct beings with a personal consciousness and will; but it is also true that he used by preference, for the inhabitants of the invisible world, such abstract titles as left their personal nature, though not their power or tendency, shrouded in some mystery.

τοὺς κοσμοκράτορας τοῦ σκότους τούτου. In ii. 2, "according to the course of this world, according to the ruler of the power of the air, the spirit now working in the children of disobedience," the singular is used, instead of the plural as here.

πρὸς τὰ πνευματικά, "the spiritualities, the spiritual forces or activities."

13. ἐν τῇ ἡμέρᾳ τῇ πονηρᾷ, "the evil day," whenever it may come.

κατεργασάμενοι *might* mean "having put down;" but Pauline usage sufficiently determines it to mean "having accomplished."

14. στῆτε. Observe the frequent repetition of the idea of *standing* in this passage, στῆναι (verse 11), ἀντιστῆναι, στῆναι (verse 13), and here again in verse 14. So in Philippians *l.c.* ὅτι στήκετε.

The images are mostly borrowed from the book of Isaiah.

For "the girdle of truth and the breastplate of righteousness" see Isa. xi. 5, καὶ ἔσται δικαιοσύνη ἐζωσμένος τὴν ὀσφῦν αὐτοῦ καὶ ἀληθείᾳ εἰλημένος τὰς πλευράς, and

15 ἐνδυσάμενοι τὸν θώρακα τῆς δικαιοσύνης, καὶ ὑποδη-
σάμενοι τοὺς πόδας ἐν ἑτοιμασίᾳ τοῦ εὐαγγελίου τῆς
16 εἰρήνης, ἐπὶ πᾶσιν ἀναλαβόντες τὸν θυρεὸν τῆς πισ-

lix. 17, καὶ ἐνεδύσατο δικαιοσύνην ὡς θώρακα. It is plain from a comparison of these passages, (in the former "righteousness" is the girdle,) that no substantial difference is intended between "righteousness" and "truth." And if the context in Isaiah be read, we see that these words are obviously used in their broad and simple sense. They denote equity, integrity, sincerity. These then are to be the great defensive weapons of Christ's soldiers. Without these their most vital parts—the affections, the will, the conscience—would be exposed to the assaults of the enemy. To withstand the spirit of falsehood, a man must be primarily true and just.

Compare τὰ ὅπλα τοῦ φωτός (Rom. xiii. 12), and διὰ τῶν ὅπλων τῆς δικαιοσύνης τῶν δεξιῶν καὶ ἀριστερῶν (2 Cor. vi. 7).

Two passages illustrative of moral armour are quoted in Bleeck's Translation of Spiegel's Zend Avesta. One is from the Minokhired, a Parsee book: "One can escape from hell if one uses heavenly wisdom as a covering for the back, heavenly contentment as armour, heavenly truth for a shield, heavenly gratitude for a club, heavenly wisdom as a bow." The other is from a Buddhist work, which says of Sakyamuni: "And converting Sīla (Virtue) into a cloak, and Jhânam (Thought) into a breastplate, he covered mankind with the armour of Dhammo (Law), and provided them with the most perfect panoply." (Bleeck, p. 90.)

15. In Isa. v. 27, "the latchet of the shoes" follows after "the girdle of the loins."

ἑτοιμασίᾳ, "preparedness," "readiness." But what is the preparedness of the glad tidings of peace?—In Rom. x. 15 we read, "How shall they preach, except they be sent? as it is written, 'How beautiful are the feet of them that bring glad tidings of peace, of them that bring glad tidings of good things!'" The quotation is from Isa. lii. 7. The same expression occurs in Nahum i. 15, "Behold upon the mountains the feet of him that bringeth glad tidings and publisheth peace." The "feet" then, we infer from these passages, are to be "ready" in the work of spreading "the glad tidings of peace." St. Paul has said above (ii. 17) of Christ, ἐλθὼν εὐηγγελίσατο εἰρήνην. A willing zeal in this task is to be as shoes to the feet of the Christian.

16. ἐπὶ πᾶσιν, "in addition to

τέως, ἐν ᾧ δυνήσεσθε πάντα τὰ βέλη τοῦ πονηροῦ
17 τὰ πεπυρωμένα σβέσαι. καὶ τὴν περικεφαλαίαν τοῦ
σωτηρίου δέξασθε, καὶ τὴν μάχαιραν τοῦ πνεύματος,

all." This sense is more in accordance with usage than "over all," and much more than "above all." See Col. iii. 14.

In the Wisdom of Solomon v. 17—20, there is a description of a πανοπλία, which not man, but the Lord, is to take to him. "He shall put on righteousness as a breastplate, and true judgment instead of an helmet. He shall take holiness for an invincible shield. His severe wrath shall he sharpen for a sword." For man, the shield, instead of being inherent holiness, is faith or trust. In the language of the Old Testament, the Lord himself is the shield of those who fear him, defending them from all evil. Here the shield of faith is for use especially against the fire-bearing darts of the evil one. Those darts are suspicions and doubts, which it is the business of the evil spirit to infuse into men's hearts,—suspicions of God and of one another. Faith, trust in God, is the exact way to meet these. He who thoroughly believes and trusts in God will be safe against the destructive effects of the doubts which the devil inspires.

τὰ πεπυρωμένα. The only "fiery dart" in use amongst the ancients appears to have been a certain heavy missile called in Latin *malleolus:* "a hammer, the transverse head of which was formed for holding pitch and tow; which, having been set on fire, was projected slowly, so that it might not be extinguished during its flight, upon houses and other buildings in order to set them on fire." (Smith's Dictionary of Antiquities, *Malleus.*) But perhaps the fire with which St. Paul's βέλη were armed was rather drawn from imagination than from reality.

17. τὴν περικεφαλαίαν τοῦ σωτηρίου. From Isa. lix. 17, καὶ περιέθετο περικεφαλαίαν σωτηρίου ἐπὶ τῆς κεφαλῆς. But there it is *the Lord* who assumes the helmet of salvation, as also the breastplate of righteousness and the garment of vengeance. So far as is possible, St. Paul transfers to the Christian the identical arms which the prophet attributes to the Lord; —and, regarded in this light, the πανοπλία τοῦ θεοῦ may mean rather more than the armour which God *gives.* But man is not God, and man's "helmet of salvation" must be different from God's. In 1 Thess. v. 8, St. Paul has already given his own interpretation of this helmet: "and, for a helmet, *the hope* of salvation." As illustrating this figure, we may quote Ps. iii. 3,

18 ὅ ἐστιν ῥῆμα θεοῦ, διὰ πάσης προσευχῆς καὶ δεήσεως προσευχόμενοι ἐν παντὶ καιρῷ ἐν πνεύματι, καὶ εἰς αὐτὸ ἀγρυπνοῦντες ἐν πάσῃ προσκαρτερήσει καὶ δεήσει 19 περὶ πάντων τῶν ἁγίων, καὶ ὑπὲρ ἐμοῦ, ἵνα μοι δοθῇ λόγος ἐν ἀνοίξει· τοῦ στόματός μου, ἐν παρρησίᾳ 20 γνωρίσαι τὸ μυστήριον τοῦ εὐαγγελίου, ὑπὲρ οὗ

"Thou, O Lord, art a shield for me; my glory, *and the lifter up of mine head;*" especially as coupled with the Sept. form of the preceding verse, Πολλοὶ λέγουσι τῇ ψυχῇ μου Οὐκ ἔστι σωτηρία αὐτῷ ἐν τῷ θεῷ αὐτοῦ. The expression "*to lift up the head*" is very common in the Old Testament.

δέξασθε, "*receive*, as a gift from God." τὴν μάχαιραν τοῦ πνεύματος, ὅ ἐστιν ῥῆμα θεοῦ. For the image compare Isa. xlix. 2, ἔθηκε τὸ στόμα μου ὡς μάχαιραν ὀξεῖαν, Rev. i. 16, ἐκ τοῦ στόματος αὐτοῦ ῥομφαία δίστομος ὀξεῖα ἐκπορευομένη, xix. 15, ἐκ τοῦ στόματος αὐτοῦ ἐκπορεύεται ῥομφαία ὀξεῖα, ἵνα ἐν αὐτῇ πατάσσῃ τὰ ἔθνη, and Heb. iv. 12, Ζῶν γὰρ ὁ λόγος τοῦ θεοῦ καὶ ἐνεργής, καὶ τομώτερος ὑπὲρ πᾶσαν μάχαιραν δίστομον. The difficulty is to attach the same meaning to *the word* or *the sword* in these different passages. Let it be remembered, 1. That the Word is to be understood as the living *voice* of God, instinct with mind and purpose, and having all the power of God's will. 2. That the Voice may have varying tones, and may either threaten wrath, or offer love. 3. That, in the habitual use of St. Paul, "the word of God" is almost equivalent to the Gospel, or God's voice proclaiming reconciliation and inviting men to peace. 4. That the image of a sharp sword represents the *penetrating* effect of God's word on the conscience, and its power to assail and destroy such spiritual enemies as darkness, distrust, and all moral evil.

Christians then, according to St. Paul's exhortation, are to use God's voice, his truth or light, as their weapon of offence. The mode of using or wielding God's word which he had chiefly in view was that of bearing witness to the truth, and especially to the most life-giving of all truths, the Gospel of Christ.

18—20. The urgent exhortation to prayer in behalf of the Church and for the diffusion of the Gospel proves how distinctly St. Paul had in his mind the warfare of Christians as that of a body fighting the battle of Christ in the world, rather than the warfare of the individual fighting for his own salvation.

20. ὑπὲρ οὗ πρεσβεύω ἐν ἁλύσει,

πρεσβείω ἐν ἁλύσει, ἵνα ἐν αὐτῷ παρρησιάσωμαι ὡς δεῖ με λαλῆσαι.

21 Ἵνα δὲ εἰδῆτε καὶ ὑμεῖς τὰ κατ' ἐμέ, τί πράσσω, πάντα ὑμῖν γνωρίσει Τύχικος ὁ ἀγαπητὸς ἀδελφὸς καὶ 22 πιστὸς διάκονος ἐν κυρίῳ, ὃν ἔπεμψα πρὸς ὑμᾶς εἰς αὐτὸ τοῦτο ἵνα γνῶτε τὰ περὶ ἡμῶν καὶ παρακαλέσῃ τὰς καρδίας ὑμῶν.

23 Εἰρήνη τοῖς ἀδελφοῖς καὶ ἀγάπη μετὰ πίστεως ἀπὸ 24 θεοῦ πατρὸς καὶ κυρίου Ἰησοῦ Χριστοῦ. ἡ χάρις μετὰ πάντων τῶν ἀγαπώντων τὸν κύριον ἡμῶν Ἰησοῦν Χριστὸν ἐν ἀφθαρσίᾳ.

"the cause of which I advocate in a chain." Compare Col. iv. 2—4.

21. Τύχικος, called Ἀσιανός in Acts xx. 4. He was a trusted helper and agent of St. Paul, and was to carry both this letter and that to the Colossians. See Col. iv. 7—9.

διάκονος, "a minister," i.e. one who ministered to St. Paul. Compare ἔστιν γάρ μοι εὔχρηστος εἰς διακονίαν (2 Tim. iv. 11).

24. ἐν ἀφθαρσίᾳ. A difficult expression. "In a spirit which corruption cannot touch," "incorruptibly."

TO THE EPHESIANS.

PAUL, an apostle of Christ Jesus by the will of God, to the saints that are at Ephesus and the faithful in Christ Jesus. Grace to you and peace from God our Father and the Lord Jesus Christ.

Blessed be God and the Father of our Lord Jesus Christ, who has blessed us with all spiritual blessing in heavenly things in Christ, according as he chose us in him before the foundation of the world, that we should be holy and blameless before him in love, having fore-ordained us to filial adoption through Jesus Christ unto himself, according to the good pleasure of his will, to the praise of the glory of his grace, with which he has favoured us in the beloved one, in whom we have redemption through his blood, the remission of our trespasses, according to the riches of his grace,—in which he has abounded towards us in all wisdom and prudence, making known to us the mystery of his will, according to his good pleasure which he purposed in him unto the dispensation of the fulness of the times, to bring all things under one head in Christ, things in the heavens and things on earth, even in him, in whom also we have had an inheritance given us, having been fore-ordained according

I. 11 to the purpose of him who works all things according
12 to the counsel of his will, so that we should be to the
13 praise of his glory, [we] who first hoped in Christ; in whom you also, having heard the word of truth, the gospel of your salvation, in whom (I say) having believed you were sealed with the Holy Spirit of promise,
14 who is the earnest of our inheritance unto the redemption of the possession, to the praise of his glory.

15 On this account I also, having heard of the faith among you in the Lord Jesus, and the love to all the
16 saints, do not cease to give thanks for you, making
17 mention of you in my prayers, that the God of our Lord Jesus Christ, the Father of glory, may give you the spirit of wisdom and revelation in the knowledge
18 of him, the eyes of your heart being enlightened, so that you may know what is the hope of his calling, and what the riches of the glory of his inheritance in
19 the saints, and what the exceeding greatness of his power towards us who believe, according to the working
20 of the might of his strength, with which he wrought in Christ when he raised him from the dead and seated
21 him at his right hand in the heavenly world, far above all rule and authority and power and lordship and every name that is named, not only in this age but
22 also in that which is to come, and put all things under his feet, and gave him to be head over all things to
23 the Church, which is his body, the fulness of him who
II. 1 fills all things in all. And you, being dead in tres-
2 passes and sins, in which you once walked according to the course of this world, according to the ruler of the power of the air, the spirit which now works in

the sons of disobedience, amongst whom we also all once lived in the lusts of our flesh, doing the desires of the flesh and of the thoughts, and were by nature children of wrath like the rest,—but God, being rich in mercy, on account of his great love with which he loved us, even when we were dead in trespasses made us alive with Christ (by grace have you been saved) and with him raised us and seated us in the heavenly world in Christ Jesus, that he might shew forth in the ages to come the exceeding riches of his grace in goodness towards us in Christ Jesus. For by grace you have been saved through faith, and this not of yourselves, the gift is God's,—not of works that no one may boast: for we are his workmanship, created in Christ Jesus for good works, which God before prepared that we should walk in them.

Wherefore remember, that at one time you Gentiles in the flesh, called the uncircumcision by what is called the circumcision in the flesh, made by hands,—that you were at that time apart from Christ, aliens from the commonwealth of Israel and strangers to the covenants of the promise, not having a hope, and without God in the world: but now in Christ Jesus you who were once afar off have been made nigh in the blood of Christ. For he is our peace, who made both one and broke down the dividing-wall of the fence, having done away the enmity in his flesh, the law of commandments in decrees, that he might create the two in himself into one new man, making peace, and might reconcile both in one body to God by means of the cross, having slain on it the enmity. And he came with glad tidings of peace to you who were far

II. 18 off and peace to them who were near, inasmuch as by him we both have our access in one Spirit to the
19 Father. So then you are no longer strangers and foreigners, but fellow-citizens with the saints, and of
20 God's household, being built up upon the foundation of the apostles and prophets, Christ Jesus being him-
21 self the corner-stone, in whom all the building fitly framed together is growing into a holy temple in the
22 Lord, in whom you also are being built up together into a dwelling-place of God in the Spirit.

III. 1 On this account I Paul, the prisoner of Jesus Christ
2 in behalf of you Gentiles,—if you have heard of the dispensation of the grace of God which was given me
3 towards you; how that by revelation was made known to me the mystery, (as I wrote before in brief words,
4 from which as you read them you may understand my
5 knowledge in the mystery of Christ,) which in other generations was not made known to the sons of men, as it has now been revealed to his holy apostles and
6 prophets in the Spirit, that the Gentiles should be joint-heirs and of the same body and sharers in the
7 promise in Christ through the gospel, of which I was made a minister according to the gift of the grace of God which was given to me according to the working
8 of his power. To me who am less than the least of all the saints was this grace given, to bear to the Gentiles the glad tidings of the unsearchable riches of Christ,
9 and to enlighten all men as to the dispensation of the mystery which from the ages had been kept
10 hidden in God the Creator of all things, in order that now to the principalities and powers in the heavenly

world might be made known through the Church the III. 10
manifold wisdom of God, according to the purpose of 11
the ages, which he formed in Christ Jesus our Lord,
in whom we have our freedom of speech and access 12
in confidence through faith in him. Wherefore I pray 13
you not to despond in my afflictions in your behalf,
which are your glory.—

—On this account I bend my knees unto the Father, 14
from whom every stock owning a common father in 15
heaven and on earth is named, that he may grant to 16
you according to the riches of his glory to be
strengthened with power by his Spirit unto the inner
man, that Christ may dwell by means of faith in 17
your hearts, so that being rooted and grounded in love
you may be enabled to comprehend with all saints what 18
is the breadth and length and depth and height, and 19
to know that love of Christ which transcends knowledge, that you may be filled up to all God's fulness.

Now to him who is able to do superabundantly in 20
excess of anything that we ask or think according to
the power that works in us, to him be glory in the 21
Church in Christ Jesus unto all the generations of the
age of the ages, Amen.

I exhort you therefore, I the prisoner in the Lord, to IV. 1
walk worthily of the calling with which you have
been called, with all humility and meekness, with long- 2
suffering, bearing from one another in love, endeavouring 3
to keep the unity of the Spirit in the bond of peace.
There is one body and one Spirit, even as you were 4
called in one hope of your calling; one Lord, one faith, 5
one baptism, one God and Father of all, who is over 6

IV. 7 all and through all and in all. But to each of us severally has his own grace been given according to
8 the measure of the gift of Christ. Wherefore it says, "Having gone up on high he made captive captivity,
9 and gave gifts unto men." But that *he went up*, what is it but that he also *came down* to the
10 lower parts of the earth? He who came down is the same who also went up far above all the heavens, that
11 he might fill all things. And he has given some to be apostles, and some prophets, and some evangelists,
12 and some shepherds and teachers, for the organizing of the saints, unto the work of ministering, unto the
13 building of the body of Christ; until we all attain to the unity of the faith and of the knowledge of the Son of God, unto the full-grown Man, unto the measure of
14 growth of the fulness of Christ; that we should no longer be childish, tossed and carried about by every wind of teaching in the craft of men in knavery, to the
15 pursuing of error; but cleaving to truth may in love grow up unto him in all things, who is the head,
16 namely Christ; from whom all the body, fitly framed together and compacted by means of every joint of the whole supply, according to the working in its measure of each several part effects the growth of the body to the building up of itself in love.
17 This I say therefore and urge upon you in the Lord, that *you* no longer walk as the rest of the Gentiles
18 walk in vanity of their understanding, being darkened in their mind, estranged from the life of God, through the ignorance that is in them, through the hardening of
19 their heart, who being past feeling have given themselves up to wantonness, unto the working of all unclean-

ness with greediness. But you have not so learned Christ: if indeed you have heard him and have been taught in him as there is truth in Jesus, that you should put off as concerns your former manner of life the old man going to ruin according to the lusts of deceit, and be renewed in the spirit of your mind, and put on the new man created according to God in righteousness and holiness of truth. IV. 20, 21, 22, 23, 24

Wherefore putting off falsehood speak the truth every one with his neighbour, inasmuch as we are members of one another. "Be angry and sin not;" let not the sun go down upon your anger, and give not room to the devil. Let the stealer steal no more, but rather let him labour, working with his hands at that which is good, that he may have somewhat to impart to him that is in need. Let no unwholesome speech proceed out of your mouth, but whatever is good for edification according to the need, that it may confer a benefit on those who hear it. And grieve not the holy Spirit of God, with which you were sealed unto the day of redemption. Let all bitterness and wrath and anger and clamour and evil speaking be put away from among you, with all malice. Shew yourselves kind to one another, tender-hearted, forgiving one another even as God in Christ has forgiven you. 25, 26, 27, 28, 29, 30, 31, 32

Be therefore imitators of God, as beloved children, and walk in love, as Christ also loved us and gave himself up for us an offering and a sacrifice to God for a smell of sweet savour. But fornication and all uncleanness, or covetousness, let it not be so much as named amongst you, as becomes a holy community, or lewdness or foolish talking or jesting, which are not seemly, V. 1, 2, 3, 4

v. 5 but rather thanksgiving. For this you have learnt and know, that every fornicator or unclean person, or covetous man, who is an idolater, has no inheritance
6 in the kingdom of Christ and God. Let no one deceive you with vain words: for on account of these things comes the wrath of God upon the sons of disobedience.
7, 8 Be not therefore partakers with them. For you were once darkness, but now you are light in the Lord,—
9 walk as children of light, (for the fruit of light is in
10 all goodness and righteousness and truth,) proving
11 what is acceptable to the Lord; and have no partnership with the barren works of darkness, but rather
12 convict them. For the things done in secret by them
13 it is a shame even to speak of. But all things when convicted are made manifest by light; for all that is
14 made manifest is light. Wherefore it says, "Awake, O sleeper, and rise from the dead, and the Christ shall shed light upon thee."

15 See then that you walk carefully, not as fools but
16 as wise men, buying up the right time, because the
17 days are evil. On this account be not unwise, but
18 understanding what the will of the Lord is. And be not drunk with wine, in which is excess, but make
19 yourselves full with the Spirit, speaking to yourselves in psalms and hymns and spiritual songs, singing and
20 making music in your hearts to the Lord, giving thanks always for all things in the name of our Lord Jesus
21 Christ to God and the Father, submitting yourselves one to another in the fear of Christ.
22 Let wives submit to their own husbands as to the
23 Lord, because the husband is the head of the wife as

Christ is the head of the Church,—*he* being the Saviour of the Body. Nevertheless, as the Church is subject to Christ, so let wives be to their husbands in everything. Husbands, love your wives, as Christ also loved the Church and gave himself up for it, that he might sanctify it through a purification in the laver of water by the word, that he might himself present the Church to himself a glorious bride, not having spot or wrinkle or any such thing, but that it should be holy and without blemish. In like manner husbands also ought to love their own wives as their own bodies. He that loves his wife loves himself. For no one ever yet hated his own flesh, but nourishes and cherishes it, even as Christ does the Church, inasmuch as we are members of his body. For this reason shall a man leave father and mother and be joined to his wife, and the two shall make one flesh. This mystery is a great one, but I, in what I am saying, refer to Christ and the Church. Only do you individually each man love his wife even as himself, and let the wife see that she fear her husband.

Children, obey your parents in the Lord; for this is right. "Honour thy father and thy mother," which is the first commandment with a promise, that it may be well with thee and thou mayest be long-lived upon the earth. And, ye fathers, provoke not your children, but bring them up in the discipline and instruction of the Lord.

Bond-servants, obey your masters according to the flesh with fear and trembling, in singleness of your heart, as obeying Christ, not with eye-service, as men-pleasers, but as bond-servants of Christ, doing the will

VI. 7 of God from the heart, rendering service with good-
8 will as to the Lord and not to men, knowing that whatever good a man do, *that* he shall receive from
9 the Lord, whether he be bondsman or free. And ye masters, do the same things to them, sparing threats, knowing that both they and you have a Master in heaven, and there is no accepting of the person with him.

10 For the rest, be strong in the Lord, and in the power
11 of his might. Put on the complete armour of God, that you may be able to stand against the devices of
12 the devil; inasmuch as our wrestling is not against flesh and blood, but against principalities, against powers, against the world-rulers of this darkness, against the spiritual forces of evil in the heavenly
13 sphere. Therefore take to yourselves the complete armour of God, that you may be able to withstand in the evil day, and having accomplished all to stand.
14 Stand therefore, having girded your loins with truth, and having put on the breastplate of righteousness,
15 and having shod your feet with the preparedness of
16 the glad tidings of peace; taking, in addition to all else, the shield of faith, with which you shall be able
17 to quench all the fire-tipt darts of the evil one: and receive the helmet of salvation, and the sword of the
18 Spirit, which is the word of God; praying with all prayer and entreaty at all times in the Spirit, and watching unto this with all perseverance and entreaty
19 for all the saints, and for me, that utterance may be given me, by the opening of my mouth, with confidence
20 to make known the mystery of the Gospel, in behalf

of which I am an ambassador in a chain, that I may v. 20 be bold in proclaiming it, as I ought to speak.

But that you also may know about me, how I 21 am faring, Tychicus the beloved brother and faithful minister in the Lord will inform you of everything, whom I have sent unto you for this very purpose, that 22 you may know about us, and that he may comfort your hearts.

Peace be to the brethren, and love with faith, from 23 God the Father and the Lord Jesus Christ. Grace 24 be with all those who love our Lord Jesus Christ incorruptibly.

INTRODUCTION TO THE EPISTLE TO THE COLOSSIANS.

IF we read the Epistle to the Colossians immediately after the Epistle to the Ephesians, a difference of style undoubtedly makes itself felt. I do not think, indeed, that the feeling of any reader will be that he is returning to a Pauline style from a style unlike St. Paul's. On the contrary, if we had to judge by style only, the Epistle to the Ephesians is rather more similar to those writings of St. Paul which are universally acknowledged as genuine than the Epistle to the Colossians. The change is from comparative freedom and fluency to a stiffer and more broken style. From some cause about which we can only make guesses, the Epistle to the Colossians is distinguished not only by a want of freedom in its composition, but also by an apparent want of finish. It reads in some places as if we had not a sound text. Two or three sentences can hardly be made to give a reasonable sense. The MSS. shew a greater than usual variety of readings, arising either out of some original uncertainty of the text, or out of the difficulty of understanding what the author meant. I refer especially to the latter half of the first chapter, and to the second chapter from the 8th verse to the end.

The two Epistles profess to have been written for the same messenger to carry (Eph. vi. 21 ; Col. iv. 7), and they agree so closely both in ideas and in particular expressions that, if one is not an imitation of the other, they are manifestly twin productions. It is difficult to explain therefore why the thoughts of the writer should have run more smoothly in the one Epistle than in the other. We must be content to say that some unknown circumstance affecting the composition and dictation of the Epistle to the Colossians has caused the style of this Epistle to appear laboured, rough, and unfinished. Whatever it may have been that had this effect, it certainly did not weaken the *substance* of the letter. That is eminently genuine and strong. The personal allusions here are full of feeling and force. The theology is more far-reaching, both as regards the nature and manifestation of God, and the relations of man to God, than in almost any other work of the Apostle.

The leading idea of the Epistle is the presentation of Christ as the Mediator between God and men, who perfectly reveals God and perfectly embodies humanity, leaving no gap to be filled up between God and the world, binding the human race to God in a spiritual fellowship such as no gradation of intermediate orders of beings, nor any efforts of religious discipline, could possibly create.

It is evident that this subject was chosen with express reference to certain needs or dangers of the Colossian Church. The Epistle contains warnings against particular forms of teaching by which the Christians of Colossæ were being misled. It was in consequence of information to this effect that the letter was written. The circumstances which gave birth to the Epistle may be described as follows.

Epaphras was a member of the Church at Colossæ, holding some office, apparently that of the chief pastor and teacher, in the Christian society (i. 7 ; iv. 12, 13). He had come to Rome, and had made a report to St. Paul of the state of his Church. It is clear that St. Paul, who had not founded, and was not personally known to, the Churches in which Epaphras was interested (ii. 1 ; iv. 13), was acknowledged as the general overseer of the Gentile

Churches, at least in those countries in which he had been the first to publish the Gospel. Long before this time, the care of all the Churches had been mentioned by him as the daily burden added to his many sufferings in the cause of Christ, (ἡ ἐπίστασίς μοι ἡ καθ' ἡμέραν, ἡ μέριμνα πασῶν τῶν ἐκκλησιῶν, 2 Cor. xi. 28.) Such reports as this of Epaphras we must suppose him to have been constantly receiving; and a part of his daily work must have consisted in communicating, either by messages or by letters, with the Churches whose affairs were thus brought before him. Epaphras was able to give in part a very favourable account of the Christian body at Colossæ. "Our brethren there," he said, "have received the Gospel with a very thorough acceptance; they are earnest in their faith, and feel themselves strongly bound in love to all their fellow-believers. Their belief is bearing good practical fruit. But certain doctrines are being disseminated with much urgency and plausibility, which, to me and those of us who are carrying on the teaching of the Apostles of Christ, do not seem to accord with the spirit of the Gospel which you proclaimed. We are uneasy about these new doctrines, and desire that our Churches should receive some instruction from you concerning them. The teachers who are introducing these novelties begin by speaking of a Knowledge (*Gnosis*) which can only be imparted to those who are specially initiated into its mysteries. They speak of 'the Fulness' (*Pleroma*), a kind of ultimate abyss of Divinity, from which more knowable forms, including that of the Christ, have emanated. They name 'principalities and powers,' which fill up the interval between the unapproachable Fulness and the human race. They prescribe rules by which a man may raise himself higher and higher towards the mysterious unseen world. Those who seek after this elevation are required to separate themselves as much as possible from the common multitude. They must adopt rigorously the exclusive principle of the Jewish Law, must make much of Circumcision and all that it involves, must observe times and seasons, must practise fasting and other kinds of mortification, and must seek by prayer and worship the aid of the heavenly mediators." In some such way, we infer from the Epistle, did the excellent Epaphras describe the condition of his Church.

These notions occur with more or less of variation in the Gnostical systems of the second century. But it gives an artificial air to the subject, to call them by the formal name of Gnosticism, and then to inquire whether Gnosticism had yet arisen in the Christian world. The most probable answer to such an inquiry would be that Gnosticism was not known in the Church till a later period than the date of the Epistle to the Colossians. But it would not be a legitimate inference that the teaching just described could not have existed at that date in Colossæ. And when we think of the notions themselves, apart from the name of Gnosticism, it is much less difficult to believe that they were then in circulation. Positive external evidence on the question is almost entirely wanting. But we have the demonstrable fact, that the systems of Gnosticism sprang from a mixture of the Christian faith with religious doctrines which prevailed before the Christian era. Not only were schemes of a Pleroma and Emanations in existence in Asia before the Christian Church was founded, but they must have been carried down by tradition in the religious or intellectual world until they were developed into the full-blown systems of the Gnostics. There is therefore no presumption against the belief that in the peculiarly fertile soil of that age the seeds of future Gnostical theories were already germinating and producing a first growth. For indeed the decay and mixture of old creeds in the Asiatic intellect had created a soil of "loose fertility,—a footfall there Sufficing to upturn to the warm air Half-germinating" theosophies. Nor is there anything unreasonable in believing that the power of Apostolic teaching and of Apostolic authority, whilst the Churches were still subject to the direct influence of that power, availed to check these misgrowths, and to postpone their day. The origin of what by anticipation we may call Gnostical doctrines is discussed more fully in the Essay at the end of this volume; here it may be sufficient to say that a meeting of the Persic or Zoroastrian religion with Judaism was sufficient to account for all the dangerous teaching referred to in the Epistle to the Colossians, and that traces of such a meeting are to be found in the Jewish literature antecedent to the time of Christ.

St. Paul was profoundly interested by the report of Epaphras, agreeing as it did with much that he was probably hearing at the same time from other sources. By the stimulus thus given to his thoughts, he became aware, may we not believe? of depths in the Gospel of Christ and of aspects of the Person of Christ which he had not so clearly apprehended before. As he heard of the Christian zeal and excellence of the believers at Colossæ and Laodicea and Hierapolis, and meditated on the errors which threatened to undermine so fair an edifice, and on the truths by which those errors might most effectually be dispelled, his concern for the Colossian brethren grew into as strong an affection as if he had known them by face, and the letter which took shape in his mind was warmed by intense personal sympathy. It is a genuine *letter*, whilst it is also an exposition of those Christian ideas which were the proper antidote to such teaching as was infesting some of the Churches of Asia Minor.

The Epistle to the Colossians may be divided, like that to the Ephesians, into two parts, the former consisting of "pure" theology, or the declaration of God's nature and acts; the latter of "applied" theology, or the drawing out of duty from the relations of men to God. This division is best made at the end of the second chapter. It is in the latter half that the resemblances between this and the sister Epistle are most abundant. From the fifth verse of the third chapter to the ninth of the fourth, there is scarcely a sentence which does not also occur, either in so many words or with some variety of expression, in the Epistle to the Ephesians. In the former half the obvious coincidences are chiefly in two or three passages relating to redemption by the death of Christ, in the utterances of thanksgiving and praise on the behalf of those who are addressed, and in the mention of the mystery long hidden but now revealed, and of the rising of Christians to a new life in the resurrection of Christ.

The special theology of this Epistle is to be found in the part between i. 15 and iii. 4; out of which however we may conveniently abstract the passage i. 23 ... ii. 5, in which St. Paul speaks of himself. The Son of God who came in the flesh is declared to be the Image of the invisible God, and the Head of all creation, but especially of redeemed humanity. Let those who talk of "the Fulness" know that the Fulness dwelt in Christ. In itself the Divine nature is unfathomable, unapproachable; but Christ enables us to behold God as the Father. And as God does not approach *us* by a gradation of principalities and powers, but has come near to us at once in the Son; so we, in our weak and corrupt humanity, have not to climb up laboriously by means of observances and self-discipline to God, but are made one with Christ, if we will accept the fellowship; and have in him through faith and submission a complete human perfection. We shall know God by contemplating Christ: we shall rise to him and have our true life by consenting to be simply members of Christ.

The theology which thus dwells on the Son of God as

the head of creation and the living force by which its order is maintained, and as the fulness and perfection of humanity, may justly be represented as specially characteristic of this Epistle; but at the same time recollections will occur to every careful student of St. Paul's writings, of places in his other Epistles in which the same doctrine is plainly, though less fully and prominently, stated or implied. St. Paul, in the Epistle to the Colossians, is not inconsistent with himself, but he approaches more nearly than elsewhere to the theology which we associate with the name of St. John. The most decided Scriptural parallel to the passages just referred to is to be found at the beginning of St. John's Gospel. From the third verse of St. John i. to the eighteenth, almost every line contains some illustration of the doctrine of the Epistle to the Colossians. It is somewhat surprising that St. Paul does not expressly apply the title of *the Word* (Λόγος) to the Son of God. Philo had written his books, and St. Paul, certainly through Apollos and probably through others, had come into direct contact with the ideas of the Alexandrian school; and it was apparently as open to him, as it was afterwards to St. John, to adopt a name which had so much congruity with the views he was expressing. With the exception however of the use of this name, the doctrine of the first chapter of St. John is in close agreement with that of St. Paul in this Epistle. In another book bearing the name of St. John there is a sentence of similar import. "To the angel of the Church in Laodicea write, These things saith the Amen, the faithful and true witness, *the beginning of the creation of God*" (Rev. iii. 14). The close connexion of the Church at Laodicea with that of Colossæ, and the probability that the Apocalypse was written a very few years after our Epistle, render the coincidence the more interesting. To these parallel passages we may add the striking words at the beginning of the Epistle to the Hebrews, "the Son ... by whom he made the worlds (or ages, τοὺς αἰῶνας) ... the brightness of his glory and the express image of his person, (ἀπαύγασμα τῆς δόξης καὶ χαρακτὴρ τῆς ὑποστάσεως αὐτοῦ,) upholding all things by the word of his power" (Heb. i. 2, 3).

It may be worth while to remind the reader, that St. Paul looks at the mystery of the universe, not from the point of view of natural science, but from that of theology. He is concerned professedly about God and man, not about the laws of nature. But the phenomena of the outer world insist upon being recognised and demand to be accounted for. Man's life is involved inextricably in perplexing relations with outward things. All systems which attempted to set forth the nature of God and to explain the life of man had offered some theory of the connexion of the natural world with God and with man. The peculiarity of St. Paul's teaching, as addressed to disciples of the school of Philo or to students of Oriental theosophy, was not so much that it suggested any new theory of the universe, but that it firmly comprehended in the Person of the Son of God all that had been imagined of creative action in the world, and of the possibilities of a human ideal. The Father, the Son, the created universe; the Father, the Son, the human family : and in each series the terms livingly united by the Spirit. This was the doctrine which St. Paul opposed to the multiplication of intermediate beings, and to schemes of spiritual self-exaltation. And, so far as it was possible, St. Paul desired his doctrine to be rigorously tested by experience. He bade his disciples *live* on the understanding that they were united to Christ and through Christ to the Father, and that all things were subject to Christ. No man ever more thoroughly intended that his highest principles should be made the ground of common life. He included the whole range of human activity within the laws of man's relation to God in Christ. He claimed all men as Christ's, and all their actions as to be done for Christ.

The investigations of natural science have started from a different point, and have had a different aim, from St. Paul's. Inquiries into the causes or connexions of phenomena have been successful in finding out laws, which it was their business to seek. They have never found God in phenomena, but it was not to be expected that they should. But after the laws have been discovered, and when lower laws have been seen to resolve themselves into higher and more comprehensive laws, the question arises, What are these laws? Whence do they come? Why do they exist?—and to this question the New Testament supplies the answer, that they are utterances of the mind of the Creator, forms which the Word of God has impressed upon things. This answer leaves natural science free to do its own work: far from assailing that work, it puts a high honour upon it. But it professes to give the human mind light and satisfaction upon points concerning which natural science has nothing to say.

Similarly with regard to ethics, or the whole theory of human life. Systems of duty may be built up by ascertaining through experience what promotes the well-being of society. Their deductions may be right; their method the New Testament, at least, will not deny to be sound. But if we ask further, What is the object of society and its well-being? What is the relation between man's work and his Maker? St. Paul is ready with a definite answer, when he teaches that the ideal of manhood is in Christ, that the Sonship of the Son is the chief law of humanity, and that God as a Father is seeking the perfection through love of mankind and of every man.

It is not easy to break up the Epistle into parts further than has been done above. Its style is marked by continuity as well as closeness and vigour, and the two great theological passages in the first and second chapters are wrought into the texture of a genuine letter. It begins with thanksgivings and prayers on behalf of the Colossians, which lead on naturally to the work and kingdom of Christ, and so to his nature and his relation to the Father and to the world and to men. At the end of the twenty-third verse of the first chapter St. Paul pauses to speak of his own apostolical task and of his interest in the spiritual condition of his readers. He returns in ii. 9, with a tone of warning, to a setting forth of the nature of Christ and of the meaning and power of his death and resurrection and ascension. In the third chapter he appeals to his readers to live as members of a Head who was in heaven, and proceeds to give warnings and practical exhortations in detail. The latter part of the fourth chapter, from verse seven to the end, contains various personal allusions.

ΠΡΟΣ ΚΟΛΑΣΣΑΕΙΣ.

I. 1 Παῦλος ἀπόστολος Χριστοῦ Ἰησοῦ διὰ θελήματος 2 θεοῦ καὶ Τιμόθεος ὁ ἀδελφὸς τοῖς ἐν Κολασσαῖς ἁγίοις καὶ πιστοῖς ἀδελφοῖς ἐν Χριστῷ. χάρις ὑμῖν καὶ εἰρήνη ἀπὸ θεοῦ πατρὸς ἡμῶν.

3 Εὐχαριστοῦμεν τῷ θεῷ πατρὶ τοῦ κυρίου ἡμῶν Ἰησοῦ Χριστοῦ πάντοτε περὶ ὑμῶν προσευχόμενοι, 4 ἀκούσαντες τὴν πίστιν ὑμῶν ἐν Χριστῷ Ἰησοῦ καὶ 5 τὴν ἀγάπην ἣν ἔχετε εἰς πάντας τοὺς ἁγίους διὰ τὴν ἐλπίδα τὴν ἀποκειμένην ὑμῖν ἐν τοῖς οὐρανοῖς, ἣν προηκούσατε ἐν τῷ λόγῳ τῆς ἀληθείας τοῦ εὐαγγε-

1. Τιμόθεος ὁ ἀδελφός. Timothy is similarly associated with St. Paul in both the Epistles to the Thessalonians, in the Second to the Corinthians, and in those to Philemon and the Philippians. If he did not accompany the Apostle in the voyage from Cæsarea to Rome, he must have joined him soon after his arrival. Of all his converts and friends there does not seem to have been one on whom St. Paul leaned so much for sympathy and assistance as on his "own son" Timothy. His habit of associating others with himself in the writing of his letters is a noticeable and characteristic one.

3, 4. Compare Eph. i. 15, 16.

5. διὰ τὴν ἐλπίδα. The faith and the love are represented as stirred up by the hope, or the thing hoped for. The Gospel came with an offer of blessing; and the hope awakened by this offer was the very beginning of the Christian life. Compare τῇ ἐλπίδι ἐσώθημεν, Rom. viii. 24; and, for "the hope laid up in the heavens," Eph. i. 11—14, 18.

τῷ λόγῳ τῆς ἀλ., "the word of truth," as in Eph. i. 13; the word of truth proclaimed by the Gospel.

⁶ λίου τοῦ παρόντος εἰς ὑμᾶς καθὼς καὶ ἐν παντὶ τῷ κόσμῳ, καί ἐστιν καρποφορούμενον καὶ αὐξανόμενον καθὼς καὶ ἐν ὑμῖν, ἀφ' ἧς ἡμέρας ἠκούσατε καὶ ⁷ ἐπέγνωτε τὴν χάριν τοῦ θεοῦ ἐν ἀληθείᾳ· καθὼς ἐμάθετε ἀπὸ Ἐπαφρᾶ τοῦ ἀγαπητοῦ συνδούλου ἡμῶν, ὅς ἐστιν πιστὸς ὑπὲρ ὑμῶν διάκονος τοῦ Χριστοῦ, ⁸ ὁ καὶ δηλώσας ἡμῖν τὴν ὑμῶν ἀγάπην ἐν πνεύματι. ⁹ Διὰ τοῦτο καὶ ἡμεῖς, ἀφ' ἧς ἡμέρας ἠκούσαμεν, οὐ παυόμεθα ὑπὲρ ὑμῶν προσευχόμενοι καὶ αἰτούμενοι ἵνα πληρωθῆτε τὴν ἐπίγνωσιν τοῦ θελήματος αὐτοῦ ¹⁰ ἐν πάσῃ σοφίᾳ καὶ συνέσει πνευματικῇ, περιπατῆσαι ὑμᾶς ἀξίως τοῦ κυρίου εἰς πᾶσαν ἀρέσκειαν, ἐν παντὶ ἔργῳ ἀγαθῷ καρποφοροῦντες καὶ αὐξανόμενοι εἰς τὴν ¹¹ ἐπίγνωσιν τοῦ θεοῦ, ἐν πάσῃ δυνάμει δυναμούμενοι κατὰ τὸ κράτος τῆς δόξης αὐτοῦ εἰς πᾶσαν ὑπομονὴν ¹² καὶ μακροθυμίαν, μετὰ χαρᾶς εὐχαριστοῦντες τῷ πατρὶ

6. τοῦ παρόντος εἰς ὑμᾶς. The two notions of coming *to* you, and being present, are combined. "Which (the Gospel) has come amongst you."

καθώς. The repetition of καθώς causes a part of the awkwardness of this roughly-constructed sentence. If καί is prefixed to ἔστιν καρπ., we must supply πάρεστιν to ἐν παντὶ τῷ κόσμῳ. But Lachmann, with some of the best MSS., reads καθὼς καὶ ἐν παντὶ τῷ κόσμῳ ἐστὶν καρποφορούμενον, κ. τ. λ.

7. ἀπὸ Ἐπαφρᾶ. Epaphras was evidently one of the chief teachers, if he was not the founder, of the Church at Colossæ. He was now with St. Paul at Rome and is called by him his "fellow-prisoner" (Philemon 23), but probably this refers only to a voluntary companionship in St. Paul's imprisonment.

9. ἵνα πληρωθῆτε τὴν ἐπίγνωσιν, "that you may be made full as to the knowledge of his will,"—that you may gain a complete knowledge.

10. περιπατῆσαι, "so that you may walk."

ἀρέσκεια is generally "complaisance" in an unfavourable sense; but here it expresses amiability, favour with God and men.

12. "Giving thanks to the Father who has called us effectually to our portion of the inherit-

τῷ ἱκανώσαντι ἡμᾶς εἰς τὴν μερίδα τοῦ κλήρου τῶν
13 ἁγίων ἐν τῷ φωτί, ὃς ἐρρύσατο ἡμᾶς ἐκ τῆς ἐξουσίας
τοῦ σκότους καὶ μετέστησεν εἰς τὴν βασιλείαν τοῦ
14 υἱοῦ τῆς ἀγάπης αὐτοῦ, ἐν ᾧ ἔχομεν τὴν ἀπολύτρωσιν,

ance of the saints in light." There is some doubt about the right reading in this clause. καλέσαντι is in some MSS. substituted for ἱκανώσαντι, in others added (with καί) before it, in others omitted. We can easily suppose that the Apostle, having written καλέσαντι, felt that a stronger word was needed to express his meaning, "—who has called us, and *enabled* us," with an emphasis on the second word. This would account for the irregular phrase ἱκανώσαντι εἰς τὴν μερίδα. Or, on the other hand, if ἱκανώσαντι only was written, it was very natural that καλέσαντι should be given as a gloss, and so come into the text. The Apostle is not speaking of the preparation of Christians on earth for a future inheritance. " The inheritance of the saints *in light*" is represented as already entered upon, being contrasted with that " power or dominion of *darkness*," from which the believers in Christ *had been* delivered. "The portion," ἡ μερίς, is the share of each in the general inheritance. Men could not have taken possession of this in their own strength. Their "sufficiency" was of God. For this use of ἱκανῶσαι, compare 2 Cor. iii. 6,

ὃς καὶ ἱκάνωσεν ἡμᾶς διακόνους καινῆς διαθήκης. The construction of the two passages would be identical, if we substituted μετόχους for εἰς τὴν μερίδα, " who has enabled us as partakers," or made us competent to be partakers. Observe that it is *" the Father"* who has given this sufficiency. The inheritance is in fact that of *sonship* to God, with all its privileges.

13. There are two opposing dominions, the one that of the powers of darkness, the other that of the kingdom of light and peace in which the Son of God reigns over his brethren. The Christians, in obeying the call of the Gospel, had been brought out of the one into the other. Compare Eph. v. 5, 8, " has no inheritance in the kingdom of Christ and of God ;" ... " you were once darkness, but now you are light in the Lord ;" and Eph. vi. 12. Passages from the Zend Avesta relating to the opposition of Angro-mainyus (Ahriman) to Ahura-mazda (Ormuzd) are given in the *Essay on foreign Elements in the Theology of these Epistles.*

14. Identical with Eph. i. 7, except that there διὰ τοῦ αἵματος αὐτοῦ is added after ἀπολύτρωσιν,

15 τὴν ἄφεσιν τῶν ἁμαρτιῶν, ὅς ἐστιν εἰκὼν τοῦ θεοῦ
16 τοῦ ἀοράτου, πρωτότοκος πάσης κτίσεως, ὅτι ἐν αὐτῷ
ἐκτίσθη τὰ πάντα τὰ ἐν τοῖς οὐρανοῖς καὶ τὰ ἐπὶ

and παραπτωμάτων occupies the place of ἁμαρτιῶν. Here, we must connect the ἀπολύτρωσις with the deliverance just mentioned. Those who were now free subjects and citizens of Christ's kingdom had found their deliverance from the dominion of darkness in receiving that forgiveness of sins which was embodied, so to speak, in Christ and his blood.

15. εἰκὼν τοῦ θεοῦ τοῦ ἀοράτου, "the *visible* image of the invisible God." The word εἰκών here seems to refer to the bodily person of Christ. In Heb. i. 3, on the other hand, the terms ἀπαύγασμα τῆς δόξης καὶ χαρακτὴρ τῆς ὑποστάσεως αὐτοῦ may probably be understood without reference to the Incarnation, as expressing the relation of the Son to the Father in the mystery of the Divine nature.

πρωτότοκος πάσης κτίσεως. The only exact *translation* of these words is "firstborn of all creation;" and from this title it might without doubt be logically inferred that the Son was a part of creation. But this phrase belongs to a class of expressions in which the strictest grammatical sense is by no means always what is meant. We do not infer from the phrase "fairest of her daughters, Eve," that Eve was one of her own daughters. And πρωτότοκος πάσης κτίσεως *might* be written by one who meant to convey that the Son was begotten *before* any part of creation. It would scarcely be maintained that St. Paul would have applied the term κτισθείς to the Son. It is a fair and natural way of explaining the words to say, that the Son, with reference to "all creation," occupied the place of "first-born." He is prior to, and at the head of, all existence. The next sentence is sufficient to correct any false impression that St. Paul was speaking of the Son as a created being.

16. ἐν αὐτῷ ἐκτίσθη τὰ πάντα. It is confessedly difficult to explain the meaning of statements like this, and it may seem wise to pass them by as expressing mysteries which we cannot pretend to fathom. Any attempt to describe by a definition that relation to God, or the Lord, or Christ, which St. Paul so often affirms in the phrase "*in him*," must necessarily be a failure. We must be content to deny ourselves a precise answer to the question, what St. Paul meant when he said, "All things were created in the Son of God," or when he said, "In God we live and move and are." But we ought

τῆς γῆς, τὰ ὁρατὰ καὶ τὰ ἀόρατα, εἴτε θρόνοι εἴτε κυριότητες εἴτε ἀρχαὶ εἴτε ἐξουσίαι. τὰ πάντα δι' 17 αὐτοῦ καὶ εἰς αὐτὸν ἔκτισται, καὶ αὐτός ἐστιν πρὸ 18 πάντων καὶ τὰ πάντα ἐν αὐτῷ συνέστηκεν, καὶ αὐτός

to go with the mind of the Apostle when he uses such language as far as any reflections we can make will enable us to go. And with that view we should probably be right in pursuing such considerations as these:

(1.) The Son of God is a living power sustaining and embracing all things. The life, the coherence, the movement, of the universe, are due to his presence.

(2.) The order of the universe is a reflection of the mind of God. "All things" not only depend on the Son of God, but they also manifest him. The invisible law of the universe, the κόσμος νοητός, is a thought of God. The relations and processes of the whole creation will be better understood by regarding them in the light of the Divine nature, and of that nature in its Filial aspect.

These doctrines are not amongst the discoveries of modern physical science. It does not belong to science either to affirm or to contradict them. But it might be possible to trace analogies and reciprocal illustrations between this theology of creation and the principles which science holds to be most certain.

εἴτε θρόνοι, κ. τ. λ., an amplification of the more frequent ἀρχαὶ καὶ ἐξουσίαι. But no distinction is to be looked for between these terms. St. Paul seems to wish to leave open the question of the real existence of such entities as formed the mythology of Oriental systems. His object is to affirm that all existences whatsoever, let them be what they might, were necessarily created by and in and for the Son of God. Compare Eph. i. 21.

τὰ πάντα δι' αὐτοῦ καὶ εἰς αὐτὸν ἔκτισται. Compare Rom. xi. 36, ἐξ αὐτοῦ καὶ δι' αὐτοῦ καὶ εἰς αὐτὸν τὰ πάντα,—said, without restriction to the Son, of God or the Lord.

17. τὰ πάντα ἐν αὐτῷ συνέστηκεν. As in the English Version, "all things in him *consist*, or are held together." Compare Ecclus. xliii. 26, ἐν λόγῳ αὐτοῦ σύγκειται πάντα.

18. That relation of Christ to *humanity* which is implied in his being the Head of the Church is always closely associated in St. Paul's mind with the action or relation of the Son of God as the fountain and support of *creation*. Compare Eph. i. 23.

ἐστιν ἡ κεφαλὴ τοῦ σώματος, τῆς ἐκκλησίας· ὅς
ἐστιν ἀρχή, πρωτότοκος ἐκ τῶν νεκρῶν, ἵνα γένηται
19 ἐν πᾶσιν αὐτὸς πρωτεύων, ὅτι ἐν αὐτῷ εὐδόκησεν
20 πᾶν τὸ πλήρωμα κατοικῆσαι καὶ δι' αὐτοῦ ἀποκα-
ταλλάξαι τὰ πάντα εἰς αὐτόν, εἰρηνοποιήσας διὰ

ὅς ἐστιν ἀρχή. It would seem that in this place the Son of God is called ἀρχή in his character as the Head of the Church rather than in his character as the Creative Word. He is the Origin from which the Church, the redeemed Body, has its derivation.

πρωτότοκος ἐκ τῶν νεκρῶν. Here also it is the Head of the Church, the risen Saviour, who is πρωτότοκος in this second sense. Above, the Son, the Image of the Father, is the Firstborn of all creation. Now he is the Firstborn, by his resurrection from the dead, of the new creation of redeemed and reconciled spirits.

ἵνα γένηται ἐν πᾶσιν αὐτὸς πρωτεύων. "That he might gain the first place for himself in all things." Christ descended in order that he might *rise* to the highest place, and so might manifestly originate a new order.

19. There are two constructions for this sentence, according as τὸ πλήρωμα is taken for an accusative or a nominative. In the former case, the rendering of the English Version is the right one, " it pleased [God or the Father]," or more exactly, " God was pleased, that in him all the Fulness should dwell." The objection to this construction is that the omission of the name of " God" as the subject is not a natural one. In the latter case πᾶν τὸ πλήρωμα is a name for the Divine Being. " For in him all the Fulness was pleased to dwell, and by him to reconcile all things to himself." In an ordinary passage of St. Paul we should not willingly admit such an expression. But when we consider how largely the Apostle has been using the language of "theosophy" in the preceding sentences, there seems to be no incongruity, as there is certainly much force, in using a term which expresses the infinity of the Divine nature in place of any personal name of God. The more lengthened phrase in ii. 9, πᾶν τὸ πλήρωμα τῆς θεότητος, does not tell directly in favour of either construction; but it shows us still further how much St. Paul's mind was dwelling on these " mystical " ideas of God's nature, and so helps to make the unusual form of expression more probable.

20. εἰρηνοποιήσας. In either case, it is *God* who has made peace through the blood of the cross of Christ. Compare Eph. ii. 16, 17, and see the note on that passage.

τοῦ αἵματος τοῦ σταυροῦ αὐτοῦ, δι' αὐτοῦ, εἴτε τὰ
21 ἐπὶ τῆς γῆς εἴτε τὰ ἐν τοῖς οὐρανοῖς. καὶ ὑμᾶς
ποτὲ ὄντας ἀπηλλοτριωμένους καὶ ἐχθροὺς τῇ διανοίᾳ
ἐν τοῖς ἔργοις τοῖς πονηροῖς, νυνὶ δὲ ἀποκατήλλαξεν
22 ἐν τῷ σώματι τῆς σαρκὸς αὐτοῦ διὰ τοῦ θανάτου,
παραστῆσαι ὑμᾶς ἁγίους καὶ ἀμώμους καὶ ἀνεγκλήτους
23 κατενώπιον αὐτοῦ, εἴ γε ἐπιμένετε τῇ πίστει τεθεμελιωμένοι καὶ ἑδραῖοι καὶ μὴ μετακινούμενοι ἀπὸ τῆς ἐλπί-
δος τοῦ εὐαγγελίου οὗ ἠκούσατε, τοῦ κηρυχθέντος ἐν
πάσῃ κτίσει τῇ ὑπὸ τὸν οὐρανόν, οὗ ἐγενόμην ἐγὼ
Παῦλος διάκονος.

δι' αὐτοῦ, "through *him*," emphatic. The blood of the cross meant Him who shed his blood, Christ dying as a self-oblation. Observe in this verse how the Apostle insists on the *universality* of the reconciliation, and on Christ being *the one medium* of it.

21. καὶ ὑμᾶς. A direct and particular application is given to the universal statement, just as in Eph. ii. 1.

ἀπηλλοτριωμένους. Comp. Eph. iv. 18, 19.

ἐν τοῖς ἔργοις τοῖς πονηροῖς. The estrangement and enmity had its seat and manifestation and nourishment in evil acts.

ἀποκατήλλαξεν. "He (that is, God, as before,) has reconciled you in the body of Christ's flesh." The sentence does not run very smoothly, and transcribers appear to have stumbled at the δέ added for emphasis to νυνί. Lachmann gives preference to the almost impossible reading ἀποκατηλλάγητε. There are other various readings, of which ἀποκαταλλαγέντες (also impossible) holds next place.

The doctrine is still the same, —that in the living person of Christ, who gave himself up to man's death and was raised again by the Father, men, as men, are reconciled to God.

22. παραστῆσαι. It is *God*, again, who presents his reconciled children before himself. Compare Eph. i. 4.

23. εἴ γε ἐπιμένετε, "if you abide in the faith,"—not rejecting that filial condition to which God has called you.

ἐν πάσῃ κτίσει. We can hardly suppose this to have been an unmeaning exaggeration. It is to be remembered, (1) that the wide diffusion of the Gospel was a point of great importance to St. Paul, as expressing so fitly that opening of God's favour to all men uni-

24 Νῦν χαίρω ἐν τοῖς παθήμασιν ὑπὲρ ὑμῶν, καὶ ἀνταναπληρῶ τὰ ὑστερήματα τῶν θλίψεων τοῦ Χριστοῦ ἐν τῇ σαρκί μου ὑπὲρ τοῦ σώματος αὐτοῦ, ὅ ἐστιν ἡ 25 ἐκκλησία, ἧς ἐγενόμην ἐγὼ διάκονος κατὰ τὴν οἰκονομίαν τοῦ θεοῦ τὴν δοθεῖσάν μοι εἰς ὑμᾶς πληρῶσαι

versally in which he gloried; and (2) that the Gospel *had* been published over a very remarkably wide area for that age. St. Paul's own work in this preaching had been wonderful in its geographical extension, as well as in other characteristics. Nevertheless the expression cannot be made out to be a strictly accurate one, nor is it necessary that it should be. St. Paul was speaking from the point of view of theology, not of statistics. Compare verses 5, 6, of this chapter.

24. *νῦν χαίρω*. MS. authority is in favour of the omission of ὅς before νῦν, but this may partly be accounted for by the similar ending of διάκονος. The sentence is considerably injured by the excision of this copula.

The feeling here expressed of joy and pride in his sufferings was habitual to St. Paul. Whilst he held it to be a general Christian privilege to "glory in tribulations," he regarded his own peculiar afflictions as a seal of his Apostleship. But the language of this verse is the most remarkable that he anywhere uses in speaking of his sufferings.

καὶ ἀνταναπληρῶ, κ.τ.λ. There is something startling in the words, "the shortcomings of the afflictions of Christ," and in St. Paul's pretensions to supply in his person what had been left wanting by Christ. But we must bring to the reading of this passage St. Paul's idea of the Head and the members. The Body was the πλήρωμα or complement of Christ (Eph. i. 23); without it he was not complete. The Church was to be built up out of sufferings,— the sufferings of Christ first, and the sufferings of his members in their turn and place; and each member, in doing his part, was supplying that which was left vacant, so to say, for him to supply. St. Paul, who knew his part in the building up of the Church to be a great one, might honestly speak of his sufferings as contributing an important complement to the total sum of the afflictions of Christ and his members.

The *ἀντί* in *ἀνταναπληρῶ* probably implies a kind of *response* on the part of the members, echoing the action of the Head.

25. *κατὰ τὴν οἰκονομίαν*. In

26 τὸν λόγον τοῦ θεοῦ, τὸ μυστήριον τὸ ἀποκεκρυμμένον ἀπὸ τῶν αἰώνων καὶ ἀπὸ τῶν γενεῶν, νυνὶ δὲ ἐφανε-
27 ρώθη τοῖς ἁγίοις αὐτοῦ, οἷς ἠθέλησεν ὁ θεὸς γνωρίσαι τί τὸ πλοῦτος τῆς δόξης τοῦ μυστηρίου τούτου ἐν τοῖς ἔθνεσιν, ὅς ἐστιν Χριστὸς ἐν ὑμῖν, ἡ ἐλπὶς τῆς δόξης,

Eph. iii. 7, the same place is filled by the words κατὰ τὴν δωρεὰν τῆς χάριτος τοῦ θεοῦ τῆς δοθείσης μοι. And in the second verse of the same chapter the equivalent phrase is τὴν οἰκονομίαν τῆς χάριτος τοῦ θεοῦ τῆς δοθείσης μοι. On the word οἰκονομία see the note on Eph. i. 10. It is here used in the second of the senses there given, and represents an appointment or commission given by the Lord to his servant Paul. It answers to δωρεά in Eph. iii. 7,— the word most commonly used to denote this commission being χάρις. This is also the sense of οἰκονομία in Eph. iii. 2.

πληρῶσαι τὸν λόγον τοῦ θεοῦ. It would seem as if St. Paul, when a word became strongly impressed on his mind, had a pleasure in using it in various senses. Πληροῦν and πλήρωμα are among the special words of these Epistles. Here, to "fill" or "fulfil" the word of God, must mean to proclaim it to the full; to fill the appointed measure in the bearing or making known of God's word.

26. Compare Eph. iii. 9.

ἐφανερώθη, written as if ὃ ἀπε-κρύφθη had gone before, instead of its equivalent, τὸ ἀποκεκρυμμένον.

27. τί τὸ πλοῦτος τῆς δόξης τοῦ μυστηρίου τούτου ἐν τοῖς ἔθνεσιν. It is instructive to compare this with the parallel phrase in Eph. i. 18, τίς ὁ πλοῦτος τῆς δόξης τῆς κληρονομίας αὐτοῦ ἐν τοῖς ἁγίοις. There is just the same kind of recurrence and variation of words which we observe as characteristic of St. Paul not only in different compositions, but in the same letter. The variation of gender in the use of πλοῦτος may be regarded as purely casual. The different expressions in either sentence are in obvious harmony with the line of thought in each passage respectively. ἐν τοῖς ἔθνεσιν, "among the Gentiles," should be referred to the whole subject,— "the wealth of the glory of this mystery;" it implies that the Gentile world was the element, in and through which this glory was realized.

ὅς [or ὅ] ἐστιν Χριστὸς ἐν ὑμῖν. The mystery, once hidden but now manifested, is "Christ in you." In the next verse, St. Paul speaks of presenting every man τέλειον ἐν Χριστῷ, Christ in you,—you

28 ὃν ἡμεῖς καταγγέλλομεν νουθετοῦντες πάντα ἄνθρωπον καὶ διδάσκοντες πάντα ἄνθρωπον ἐν πάσῃ σοφίᾳ, ἵνα παραστήσωμεν πάντα ἄνθρωπον τέλειον ἐν Χριστῷ· 29 εἰς ὃ καὶ κοπιῶ ἀγωνιζόμενος κατὰ τὴν ἐνέργειαν αὐτοῦ τὴν ἐνεργουμένην ἐν ἐμοὶ ἐν δυνάμει.

II. 1 Θέλω γὰρ ὑμᾶς εἰδέναι ἡλίκον ἀγῶνα ἔχω περὶ ὑμῶν καὶ τῶν ἐν Λαοδικείᾳ καὶ ὅσοι οὐχ ἑώρακαν 2 τὸ πρόσωπόν μου ἐν σαρκί, ἵνα παρακληθῶσιν αἱ καρδίαι αὐτῶν, συμβιβασθέντες ἐν ἀγάπῃ καὶ εἰς πᾶν τὸ πλοῦτος τῆς πληροφορίας τῆς συνέσεως, εἰς

in Christ. We are reminded of our Lord's own saying (St. John xv. 4) μείνατε ἐν ἐμοί, κἀγὼ ἐν ὑμῖν. Such a spiritual relation to Christ is implied as may be expressed by either phrase, *Christ dwells in us*, or, *We dwell in Christ;* or best by *both* these phrases. "We are one with Christ and Christ with us." This close fellowship with Christ is the revealed mystery of God's eternal purpose, and it constitutes the hope of glory yet to be manifested.

28. The repetition of πάντα ἄνθρωπον in this verse is what chiefly attracts attention. We may trace it to that thought of *universality and completeness* which has become a passion in the Apostle's mind. He saw everything on the largest scale, but yet felt that no individual part was insignificant or to be neglected. The mystery of Christ was for the whole universe, for mankind universally; but each individual person needed to receive the mystery, to be instructed, to be informed, to be brought to a condition of personal perfection

29. And the effort to do his part in this work called for all the energetic labour which St. Paul, or the power of God in him, could put forth.

II. 1. ἡλίκον ἀγῶνα ἔχω. Referring to ἀγωνιζόμενος in the preceding verse. Compare iv. 13. The fact of not being known by face to the believers at Colossæ and Laodicea adds a kind of hungry yearning to the Apostle's desire for their spiritual welfare. From iv. 16 it appears that there was familiar intercourse between the Churches here mentioned.

2. συμβιβασθέντες. In construction, this word agrees with the supposed subject of the preceding clause;—it is expressed as if " that *they* might be comforted "

3 ἐπίγνωσιν τοῦ μυστηρίου τοῦ θεοῦ, ἐν ᾧ εἰσὶν πάντες οἱ θησαυροὶ τῆς σοφίας καὶ τῆς γνώσεως ἀπόκρυφοι.
4 τοῦτο δὲ λέγω ἵνα μηδεὶς ὑμᾶς παραλογίζηται ἐν
5 πιθανολογίᾳ. εἰ γὰρ καὶ τῇ σαρκὶ ἄπειμι, ἀλλὰ τῷ πνεύματι σὺν ὑμῖν εἰμί, χαίρων καὶ βλέπων ὑμῶν τὴν τάξιν καὶ τὸ στερέωμα τῆς εἰς Χριστὸν πίστεως
6 ὑμῶν. Ὡς οὖν παρελάβετε τὸν Χριστὸν Ἰησοῦν

had gone before. For the idea, compare Eph. iv. 13—16. Advance in *knowledge* is made dependent upon growth in Christian life,—that is, in the love and fellowship which bind the members of a true Body together.

τοῦ θεοῦ. There is a great confusion in the MSS. as to the reading here. The words θεοῦ, πατρός, and Χριστοῦ, are variously connected or omitted. The readings of the best MSS. are as follows: τοῦ θεοῦ Χριστοῦ, B, received by Lachmann; τοῦ θεοῦ πατρὸς Χριστοῦ, the Sinaitic; τοῦ θεοῦ πατρὸς τοῦ Χριστοῦ, A. C. These readings do not differ in sense from one another, if Χριστοῦ be taken as in apposition to τοῦ μυστηρίου. The mystery *is* Christ, as in i. 27, "unto the knowledge of the mystery of God (or, of God the Father), namely, Christ."

3. The words σοφία, γνῶσις, θησαυροὶ ἀπόκρυφοι, have a strongly *Gnostical* stamp, like other terms which follow in this chapter; and we cannot but conclude that St. Paul is quoting or borrowing them from theosophical speculations by which, in his judgment, the Colossian brethren were in danger of being misled. Yet the thought is almost identical with what we find in other Epistles, as for example in 1 Cor. i. 24, 30; ii. 2, 7; in the last of which places we have λαλοῦμεν θεοῦ σοφίαν ἐν μυστηρίῳ τὴν ἀποκεκρυμμένην.

4. St. Paul's earnest protest, by which he hoped to guard the Colossians against plausible false teachers, was this,—that all the γνῶσις of which they spoke, including whatever was most hidden or mystical, was *in Christ*, and was to be learnt through the study of him.

5. This assurance, interposed in the midst of an anxious exhortation, is highly characteristic of St. Paul, and shows the teacher not afraid to use his personal authority, wishing to commend rather than to censure, and bringing forward the good points in his readers which he sought to strengthen against the dangers besetting them.

7 τὸν κύριον, ἐν αὐτῷ περιπατεῖτε, ἐρριζωμένοι καὶ ἐποικοδομούμενοι ἐν αὐτῷ καὶ βεβαιούμενοι τῇ πίστει καθὼς
8 ἐδιδάχθητε, περισσεύοντες ἐν αὐτῇ ἐν εὐχαριστίᾳ. βλέπετε μή τις ἔσται ὑμᾶς ὁ συλαγωγῶν διὰ τῆς φιλο-
σοφίας καὶ κενῆς ἀπάτης κατὰ τὴν παράδοσιν τῶν
ἀνθρώπων, κατὰ τὰ στοιχεῖα τοῦ κόσμου καὶ οὐ κατὰ
9 Χριστόν, ὅτι ἐν αὐτῷ κατοικεῖ πᾶν τὸ πλήρωμα τῆς
10 θεότητος σωματικῶς καί ἐστε ἐν αὐτῷ πεπληρωμένοι, ὅς

7. ἐποικοδομούμενοι. The present tense ought to be noticed,—"in process of being built up,"— as συνοικοδομεῖσθε in Eph. ii. 22.

8. κατὰ τὴν παράδοσιν τῶν ἀνθρώπων. St. Paul's language seems to imply that there was no absolute *novelty* in the speculations offered to the Colossians. They were probably in the main *traditions*, and commended by their supporters as having the authority of tradition.

τὰ στοιχεῖα τοῦ κόσμου, also in verse 20. Compare the "weak and beggarly rudiments" of Gal. iv. 9.

9. The passage which follows is one of the most difficult in the New Testament, partly on account of the want of finish in the construction,—the connexion of clauses being especially imperfect and uncertain,—and partly on account of the mystical character of the ideas expressed. It may safely be inferred that St. Paul has in his mind *Judaistic* doctrine relating to circumcision, festivals, abstinence, and the like, and also "gnostical" doctrine (to use a later term) concerning the πλήρωμα and the heavenly orders. And most probably both kinds of doctrine were combined in the speculations of the same teachers. The Apostle subjects all such theories to the doctrine of *Christ;*—of Christ fully Divine, truly human, manifested by death and resurrection, uniting all mankind directly to God.

κατοικεῖ, "*dwells*," not "dwelt."

10. καί ἐστε ἐν αὐτῷ πεπληρωμένοι. A parenthetic clause, due to the impression made on St. Paul's mind by the word and thought of "*fulness.*" "The fulness of the Godhead is in Christ, —and your fulness also (in a true but not quite the same sense) is in him." The perfection of God and the perfection of man meet in Christ. In Christ men have their complete ideal; in proportion as they dwell in him they become perfect.

ἀρχῆς καὶ ἐξ. As in verse 15, i. 16; Eph. iii. 10.

11 ἐστιν ἡ κεφαλὴ πάσης ἀρχῆς καὶ ἐξουσίας, ἐν ᾧ καὶ περιετμήθητε περιτομῇ ἀχειροποιήτῳ, ἐν τῇ ἀπεκδύσει τοῦ σώματος τῆς σαρκός, ἐν τῇ περιτομῇ τοῦ Χριστοῦ,
12 συνταφέντες αὐτῷ ἐν τῷ βαπτίσματι, ἐν ᾧ καὶ συνηγέρθητε διὰ τῆς πίστεως τῆς ἐνεργείας τοῦ θεοῦ τοῦ
13 ἐγείραντος αὐτὸν ἐκ τῶν νεκρῶν· καὶ ὑμᾶς νεκροὺς

11. In all probability, as has been said above, some Judaistic enforcement of circumcision gave occasion to what St. Paul says here.

It is to be borne in mind that, to St. Paul, the essential reality of all spiritual relations was that mystical order, that Divine organization, which subsisted in Christ. All sacramental symbols derived their meaning and worth from the reality which they represented,—a reality on which they were dependent, but which was not dependent upon them. The strength of this feeling in St. Paul's mind enabled him to use sacred symbols for the purpose of illustration with greater freedom than is natural to us. In this passage, the circumcision of Christ and the baptism of the Christian are both appealed to as external facts which give expression and body to the great mystical laws of spiritual fellowship with Christ.

ἐν ᾧ καὶ περιετμήθητε. "In Christ you were circumcised." When?—"When *he* was circumcised." "In his circumcision, believe that you had the sins of your flesh stripped off." Again, "You have been buried with Christ." When? "In your baptism." "Believe that you then died with Christ and rose again with Christ." It would have been equally Pauline to say, "You were buried when Christ was buried, and you rose again when Christ rose again," as to say, "You went down into death with Christ when you went under the water, and rose up alive with him when you came out of the water." The historical facts of Christ's life, and the sacred symbols of the Christian life, are equally, though not in an identical manner, *expressions* of the Divine law or will which governs the higher existence of man.

12. διὰ τῆς πίστεως ... The rising to life only becomes *actual* through faith. "Believe in that putting forth of Divine Will which wrought when God raised Christ from the dead, and you also are raised again." Compare Eph. i. 19, 20, and the notes on that passage.

13. The clauses which follow resemble very closely Eph. ii. 1, 5, 14, 15, 16.

ὄντας ἐν τοῖς παραπτώμασιν καὶ τῇ ἀκροβυστίᾳ τῆς σαρκὸς ὑμῶν, συνεζωοποίησεν ὑμᾶς σὺν αὐτῷ, χαρι-
14 σάμενος ἡμῖν πάντα τὰ παραπτώματα, ἐξαλείψας τὸ καθ᾿ ἡμῶν χειρόγραφον τοῖς δόγμασιν ὃ ἦν ὑπεναντίον ἡμῖν, καὶ αὐτὸ ἦρκεν ἐκ τοῦ μέσου, προσηλώσας αὐτὸ
15 τῷ σταυρῷ, ἀπεκδυσάμενος τὰς ἀρχὰς καὶ τὰς ἐξουσίας ἐδειγμάτισεν ἐν παρρησίᾳ, θριαμβεύσας αὐτοὺς ἐν αὐτῷ.

14. In the parallel passage Eph. ii. 15, the written law, the system of decrees, is represented primarily as a barrier between Jews and Gentiles: here it is primarily a barrier between men and God. By its power to *condemn* it repels men from God. Christ by the reconciliation displayed in him has effaced all the separative power of the Law.

ἐκ τοῦ μέσου, "from the midst," *i.e.* from intervening between us and God.

15. The difficulty of connecting this verse with what goes before, through the absence of a copula, is trifling compared with the difficulty of translating and understanding the words themselves.

What is the sense of ἀπεκδυσάμενος?

What were the ἀρχαί and ἐξουσίαι to be triumphed over in Christ's work of redemption through sacrifice?

It is almost better to give up the word ἀπεκδυσάμενος in despair, than to render it "having spoiled." It is not that St. Paul was in-capable of bad grammar; but that there is no conceivable reason for his using a common word in a totally false sense. His use of ἀπέκδυσις, a very few lines above, in its right sense, makes such a false application of ἀπεκδυσάμενος still more incredible. To render it "having spoiled" is not simply to assume that the middle is wrongly used for the active voice. In the active ἀπεκδῦσαι would be to strip off *clothes*, not to strip the *body* of clothes. The ἀρχαί and ἐξουσίαι would still be stripped off, not spoiled.

Then, what are these ἀρχαί and ἐξουσίαι? It is said, *evil* powers, devils. And this interpretation is supported by Eph. vi. 12. But just above, Christ is spoken of as *the head* of all principalities and powers. And it is certainly usual in these Epistles to find ἀρχαί and ἐξουσίαι used in a neutral or comprehensive sense.

The most prudent course would perhaps be to leave the passage uninterpreted, as apparently unfinished and therefore obscure.

16 Μὴ οὖν τις ὑμᾶς κρινέτω ἐν βρώσει καὶ ἐν πόσει ἢ
17 ἐν μέρει ἑορτῆς ἢ νουμηνίας ἢ σαββάτων, ἅ ἐστιν σκιὰ

The *literal* rendering is to say that "God in Christ" stripped off from himself the principalities and powers, and made a show of them. May some such thought as this be indicated?—"False teachers are enveloping and smothering the person of Christ with a cloud of ethereal beings. But I say that Christ, in the glory of his cross, stripped himself clear of all that cloud. He rose up into a higher sphere, and placed himself distinctly above all powers of the invisible world." So it is said in Eph. iv. 10 that Christ rose "far above all heavens," and in Eph. i. 21 that God "placed him far above all ἀρχαί and ἐξουσίαι."

There is an idea of *hostility*, it is true, expressed in the words ἐδειγμάτισεν and θριαμβεύσας. If the ἀρχαί and ἐξουσίαι be regarded as in some way connected with the administration of the *Law*, (compare what is said of "angels" in Gal. iii. 19, Acts vii. 53, and Hebrews ii. 2,) a victory over *them* might be spoken of in connexion with a victory over the Law. Or, if they are simply regarded as powers which hid Christ from men, Christ in clearing himself from them might be said to vanquish them as rivals.

ἐν αὐτῷ. Probably "in him;" not "in it," viz. the cross. All through the sentence *God* in Christ is the subject.

16—23. This passage carries on the warning begun in the 8th verse. The believers were in danger of being robbed of their freedom and life given to them in Christ by being brought under a complicated system of observances. The Apostle exhorts them to refuse to be thus degraded. The language of this paragraph presents to us a succession of difficulties, including some uncertainties of text, which strengthen that impression of crudeness in the composition which is conveyed by some preceding passages. It may be supposed, perhaps, that St. Paul's dictation did not always take place under equally favourable circumstances.

16. Μὴ οὖν τις ὑμᾶς κρινέτω. You are made alive and exalted with Christ: *therefore* do not submit to be treated as subjects of a lower dispensation, bound by an external religion.

ἐν μέρει, "with reference to," "in the matter of." μέρος was used for "what concerns," as τοὐμὸν μέρος, so far as relates to me.

σαββάτων, though plural, may mean a single Sabbath. Compare St. Matthew xxviii. 1, &c.

17. Ceremonial institutions were

18 τῶν μελλόντων, τὸ δὲ σῶμα Χριστοῦ. μηδεὶς ὑμᾶς καταβραβευέτω θέλων ἐν ταπεινοφροσύνῃ καὶ θρησκείᾳ τῶν ἀγγέλων, ἃ μὴ ἑώρακεν ἐμβατεύων, εἰκῆ φυσιού-
19 μενος ὑπὸ τοῦ νοὸς τῆς σαρκὸς αὐτοῦ, καὶ οὐ κρατῶν τὴν κεφαλήν, ἐξ οὗ πᾶν τὸ σῶμα διὰ τῶν ἁφῶν καὶ συνδέσμων ἐπιχορηγούμενον καὶ συμβιβαζόμενον αὔξει
20 τὴν αὔξησιν τοῦ θεοῦ. Εἰ ἀπεθάνετε σὺν Χριστῷ ἀπὸ

but a shadow of the substance signified by them. As Christ, the substance of the Jewish institutions, had come, τὰ μέλλοντα is probably to be understood of things which *had been* "future" when the ceremonies were instituted.

τὸ σῶμα. "The body is [the body] of Christ." Σῶμα is used in a twofold sense. The Person of Christ is the body or substance of which these institutions are shadows.

καταβραβευέτω. This word means properly to decide against a person's claim to a prize. It is difficult to say whether the idea of *defrauding* is here to take precedence of that of *condemning*. If so, the βραβεῖον might be fellowship with Christ. Compare Philippians iii. 14, εἰς τὸ βραβεῖον τῆς ἄνω κλήσεως τοῦ θεοῦ ἐν Χριστῷ Ἰησοῦ.

θέλων, "at his will" or pleasure. ἐν ταπ., preaching humility, &c.

θρησκείᾳ τῶν ἀγγέλων, "worship paid to angels;" not, as some have understood it, "angelical devotion." Such devotion does not appear to have been one of the dangers which St. Paul was contemplating, nor would it have been well expressed by θρησκεία. Worship of *angels* is contrasted with holding *the Head*.

ἃ μὴ ἑώρακεν ἐμβατεύων, "entering upon, or going into, things which he has not seen,"—such as, by his theories, he might be supposed to have seen, but has not. The other reading ἃ ἑώρ., which has almost better MS. authority, cannot be made to give any tolerable meaning. Compare the following expressions in Philo: Τί, φησιν, ὦ θαυμάσιοι, τοσοῦτον αἰφνίδιον ἀρθέντες ἀπὸ γῆς εἰς ὕψος ἐπινήχεσθε καὶ τὸν ἀέρα ὑπερκύψαντες αἰθεροβατεῖτε; (i. 465.)

19. Compare Eph. iv. 16, and note. τὴν αὔξησιν τοῦ θεοῦ, "the growth which God designs and grants."

20. στοιχεῖα τοῦ κόσμου. As in verse 8, "Christ" and "the elements of the world" are put in opposition to one another. The elements of the world are here, as in Galatians iv. 9, chiefly rules of an external and superficial nature relating to observances.

τῶν στοιχείων τοῦ κόσμου, τί ὡς ζῶντες ἐν κόσμῳ 21 δογματίζεσθε Μὴ ἅψῃ μηδὲ γεύσῃ μηδὲ θίγῃς, ἅ 22 ἐστιν πάντα εἰς φθορὰν τῇ ἀποχρήσει, κατὰ τὰ ἐντάλ- 23 ματα καὶ διδασκαλίας τῶν ἀνθρώπων; ἅτινά ἐστιν λόγον μὲν ἔχοντα σοφίας ἐν ἐθελοθρησκείᾳ καὶ ταπεινοφροσύνῃ καὶ ἀφειδίᾳ σώματος, οὐκ ἐν τιμῇ τινὶ πρὸς πλησμονὴν τῆς σαρκός.

22. ἅ ἐστιν εἰς φθοράν. The objects to which the rules Touch not, &c. refer are those creatures of God which are made to be used and done with. Some have thought that it is of these rules themselves that St. Paul says that they are meant to perish in the using; which would be an instructive observation, but seems less natural than the sense commonly received.

23. This verse, though not perfectly symmetrical in construction, would have no great difficulty except for the apparently unsuitable meaning of πλησμονήν. Those rules of abstinence, says St. Paul, have a pretension of wisdom in the voluntary devotion and humility and unsparing usage of the body which they prescribe, but are not in any honour, or of any value, to the satiating of the flesh. But they were never intended to satiate the flesh; and why should that object be thought desirable? Πλησμονή so certainly denotes *more* than legitimate satisfaction, that I confess I cannot conceive it to have been used by St. Paul in a good sense. We seem to want some word meaning "effectual conquest" rather than "repletion." The flesh was to be subjugated, according to the doctrine of St. Paul as well as of the Gnostical or Judaizing teachers: the question was whether ἔργον went with λόγος, whether formal rules of abstinence *really* subdued the flesh. "Those rules are plausible," says St. Paul; we expect him to go on to say that they are delusive. The nearest approach to such a sense would be by putting some force upon πρός, and understanding it to mean "with reference to," *i.e.* "so as to withstand or overcome." Another solution is to leave the sentence without any *apodosis* answering to μέν, and to make οὐκ ἐν τιμῇ κ.τ.λ. a development of ἀφειδίᾳ σώματος, "not giving any honour to the flesh to the satisfying of it." A third explanation is to separate πρὸς πλ. from ἐν τιμῇ τινί, and render it "tending (but really tend) to the satiating of the flesh." But there is something very forced in all these interpretations.

III. 1 Εἰ οὖν συνηγέρθητε τῷ Χριστῷ, τὰ ἄνω ζητεῖτε,
2 οὗ ὁ Χριστός ἐστιν ἐν δεξιᾷ τοῦ θεοῦ καθήμενος· τὰ
3 ἄνω φρονεῖτε, μὴ τὰ ἐπὶ τῆς γῆς. ἀπεθάνετε γάρ, καὶ ἡ ζωὴ ὑμῶν κέκρυπται σὺν τῷ Χριστῷ ἐν τῷ θεῷ·
4 ὅταν ὁ Χριστὸς φανερωθῇ, ἡ ζωὴ ἡμῶν, τότε καὶ ὑμεῖς σὺν αὐτῷ φανερωθήσεσθε ἐν δόξῃ.

In this difficulty, it may be excusable to mention a conjectural emendation, although conjectural emendations are rightly excluded from the text of Scripture. If we were to read ἐπιλησμονήν, "forgetfulness," for πλησμονήν, we should get, I think, a very good sense. It is just the failure of ascetic rules, that they do not tend to a *forgetting* of the flesh. Ἐπιλησμονή is a Hellenistic word, being used by St. James (i. 25) and in the LXX. St. Paul, in a passage which has some resemblance to what we are now reading, uses the expression τὰ μὲν ὀπίσω ἐπιλανθανόμενος (Phil. iii. 13). A change from ἐπιλ. to πλ., not very violent for the copyist, would be easier to one writing from dictation, and the word σαρκός might half suggest to the ear the congenial πλησμονή.

III. 1. St. Paul assumes that the believers *had* risen with Christ. Compare ii. 12, συνταφέντες αὐτῷ ἐν τῷ βαπτίσματι, ἐν ᾧ καὶ συνηγέρθητε. This co-rising with Christ was involved in his being the Head. When the Head rose, the members also rose. But the rising was expressed, and wrought into the life of the individual, in Baptism.

The passage beginning with this verse is a very striking exposition of the highest Pauline doctrine of fellowship with Christ. We are again reminded of Philippians iii., where we have the expressions τὰ ἐπίγεια φρονοῦντες· ἡμῶν γὰρ τὸ πολίτευμα ἐν οὐρανοῖς ὑπάρχει, vv. 19, 20. St. Paul would carry out to the utmost his principle, that in the descending and ascending of Christ was laid the true basis for each man of his regenerate life. "Consider yourselves to have died, risen, and ascended to heaven, with Christ; and live now the life of those who are properly living, not on the earth, but with Christ in heaven."

3, 4. κέκρυπται. φανερωθῇ. "Now, this heavenly life must be content to be, in its inward consciousness, hidden from the world, as Christ is hidden from the world. When the veil is withdrawn from Christ, it will also be withdrawn from your membership with him."

5 Νεκρώσατε οὖν τὰ μέλη τὰ ἐπὶ τῆς γῆς, πορνείαν, ἀκαθαρσίαν, πάθος, ἐπιθυμίαν κακήν, καὶ τὴν πλεο-
6 νεξίαν ἥτις ἐστὶν εἰδωλολατρεία, δι' ἃ ἔρχεται ἡ ὀργὴ
7 τοῦ θεοῦ. ἐν οἷς καὶ ὑμεῖς περιεπατήσατέ ποτε ὅτε
8 ἐζῆτε ἐν τούτοις· νυνὶ δὲ ἀπόθεσθε καὶ ὑμεῖς τὰ πάντα, ὀργὴν θυμὸν κακίαν βλασφημίαν αἰσχρολογίαν ἐκ τοῦ
9 στόματος ὑμῶν, μὴ ψεύδεσθε εἰς ἀλλήλους, ἀπεκδυ-

5. τὰ μέλη ὑμῶν. These "*members*" are explained to be evil affections and habits. Habits form parts of a *body*, with which the inward life clothes itself. Compare ὅτε ἐζῆτε ἐν τούτοις, ver. 7.

Compare verses 5 and 6 with Eph. v. 5, 6.

6. The received text, which adds the words "upon the children of disobedience," is supported by the Sinai MS.

7. ἐν οἷς καὶ ὑμεῖς περιεπατήσατέ ποτε ὅτε ἐζῆτε ἐν τούτοις. The "walking" refers rather to the outward conduct, the "living" to inward habits and relations. Compare Gal. v. 25, εἰ ζῶμεν πνεύματι, πνεύματι καὶ στοιχῶμεν.

8. καὶ ὑμεῖς. In verse 7 "you also" meant "you, like the rest of the heathen or children of disobedience." Here it should mean "you, as others have done." But, as there has been no recent reference to Christian converts, καὶ ὑμεῖς in this verse may be only an echo of καὶ ὑμεῖς in the preceding verse.

τὰ πάντα, "the whole of them," —a more summary expression (without ταῦτα) for "all those habits."

βλασφημίαν, not limited, like our word "blasphemy," to reproaches against *God*, but, generally, all abusive language.

9. μὴ ψεύδεσθε. Lying was natural to a condition in which every man was supposed to be set against his neighbour, but unnatural to one in which unity and not division was the law.

It is interesting to compare this passage with the parallel one in Ephesians (iv. 22—25). The ideas of "the old man" and "the new man," of "putting off" and "putting on" are the same in both passages. But here the putting off and putting on are presented as already done; there, as rather *to be* done, because involved in the knowing of Christ. In Ephesians, the present participle φθειρόμενον, on the one side, answers to the present participle ἀνακαινούμενον on the opposite side in this Epistle. The old man is being destroyed, the new man is being renewed. In Ephesians, knowledge is made the *cause* or beginning of the

σάμενοι τὸν παλαιὸν ἄνθρωπον σὺν ταῖς πράξεσιν
10 αὐτοῦ καὶ ἐνδυσάμενοι τὸν νέον τὸν ἀνακαινούμενον
11 εἰς ἐπίγνωσιν κατ' εἰκόνα τοῦ κτίσαντος αὐτόν, ὅπου
οὐκ ἔνι Ἕλλην καὶ Ἰουδαῖος, περιτομὴ καὶ ἀκροβυστία,
βάρβαρος, Σκύθης, δοῦλος, ἐλεύθερος, ἀλλὰ τὰ πάντα
καὶ ἐν πᾶσιν Χριστός.
12 Ἐνδύσασθε οὖν ὡς ἐκλεκτοὶ τοῦ θεοῦ ἅγιοι καὶ
ἠγαπημένοι σπλάγχνα οἰκτιρμοῦ, χρηστότητα, ταπεινο-

change; here, it is made the *end* of it (εἰς ἐπίγνωσιν).

11. ὅπου. The antecedent to ὅπου is the dispensation or constitution implied in the preceding sentence. "In the society of the new creation there is no distinction between Greek and Jew." Compare Romans x. 12, οὐ γάρ ἐστιν διαστολὴ Ἰουδαίου τε καὶ Ἕλληνος· ὁ γὰρ αὐτὸς κύριος πάντων.

ἀλλὰ τὰ πάντα καὶ ἐν πᾶσιν Χριστός. The corresponding phrase just quoted, ὁ αὐτὸς κύριος πάντων, has not the Pauline depth of this. The new society is the Body of Christ. In and to his Body Christ is everything. Distinctions of race and condition are absorbed in the new relation. In more ordinary language we might have said, "We no longer call this man a Gentile, that man a Jew, this man barbarian, that man civilized; all are Christians, and all our significant characteristics are Christian." For "Christian" St. Paul more forcibly says "Christ." "Everything, in the new creation, is Christ: Christ is in all." Compare τοῦ μυστηρίου τούτου, ὅς ἐστιν Χριστὸς ἐν ὑμῖν, ἡ ἐλπὶς τῆς δόξης (i. 27); and ἄχρις οὗ μορφωθῇ Χριστὸς ἐν ὑμῖν, Gal. iv. 19.

12. ὡς ἐκλεκτοὶ τοῦ θεοῦ ἅγιοι καὶ ἠγαπημένοι. There can be no question that ἅγιοι καὶ ἠγ. are not in the vocative case. But it may be doubted whether ἐκλεκτοί is to be taken by itself, or characterizes ἅγιοι or both it and ἠγαπημένοι. In any case ἠγαπημένοι will be "loved" not by St. Paul, but by God. It is perhaps most in accordance with Pauline usage to understand ἅγιοι only as dependent upon ἐκλεκτοί. The meaning will thus be, "as those whom God has chosen to be holy and has loved;" "as God's chosen saints, and beloved of God." The expressions are then very similar to those in Romans i. 9, τοῖς ἐν Ῥώμῃ ἀγαπητοῖς θεοῦ, κλητοῖς ἁγίοις.

σπλάγχνα οἰκτιρμοῦ. The word σπλάγχνα in its literal sense hardly means *bowels*. It was used to describe such inward parts as the heart, the lungs, and the liver. These parts in sacrificial victims

¹³ φροσύνην, πραΰτητα, μακροθυμίαν, ἀνεχόμενοι ἀλλήλων καὶ χαριζόμενοι ἑαυτοῖς ἐάν τις πρός τινα ἔχῃ μομφήν, καθὼς καὶ ὁ Χριστὸς ἐχαρίσατο ὑμῖν οὕτως ¹⁴ καὶ ὑμεῖς, ἐπὶ πᾶσιν δὲ τούτοις τὴν ἀγάπην, ὅ ἐστιν ¹⁵ σύνδεσμος τῆς τελειότητος. καὶ ἡ εἰρήνη τοῦ Χριστοῦ βραβευέτω ἐν ταῖς καρδίαις ὑμῶν, εἰς ἣν καὶ ἐκλήθητε ¹⁶ ἐν ἑνὶ σώματι· καὶ εὐχάριστοι γίνεσθε. Ὁ λόγος τοῦ

were distinguished from the bowels, —the *viscera thoracis* from the *viscera abdominis*. See Liddell and Scott's Lexicon. The word "heart" therefore more nearly corresponds to σπλάγχνα than "bowels." It denotes the seat of tender natural feeling. The affections enumerated in this verse are the mutual duties incumbent on true members of the Body of Christ, the discharge of which will preserve the proper unity of the Body.

13. ἀνεχόμενοι ἀλλήλων. See note on Eph. iv. 2, in which verse some of the expressions of this passage are found. But the place in Ephesians which most nearly corresponds to this is iv. 24—32.

ὁ Χριστός. It is doubtful whether this, or ὁ Κύριος, be the right reading.

14. ἐπὶ πᾶσιν δὲ τούτοις. In this place, as in Eph. vi. 16, ἐπὶ πᾶσιν ἀναλαβόντες τὸν θυρεὸν τῆς πίστεως, there is some inducement to take ἐπί in the sense "over," "to cover." But it means more properly "in addition to." "Add to all these love."

ὅ ἐστιν σύνδεσμος τῆς τελειότητος, "which is the binding together of perfectness." The less precise reference of ὅ (instead of ἥ) to ἀγάπην ought to be marked. We may take "the putting on of love" as the antecedent to ὅ.

15. ἡ εἰρήνη τοῦ Χριστοῦ βραβευέτω. Compare Philip. iv. 7, ἡ εἰρήνη τοῦ θεοῦ φρουρήσει τὰς καρδίας ὑμῶν. "The peace *of Christ*" recalls the saying of our Lord, "*My* peace I give you" (St. John xiv. 27). Both here and in the passage quoted from Philippians St. Paul uses an uncommon expression to describe the dominion of peace. "Let the peace of Christ decide differences, exercise authority, in your hearts." "The peace of God shall garrison your hearts." We may more easily realize this active power of Christ's peace by thinking of Christ himself as shedding abroad his peace in the heart, and making it prevail over all dissension. Verses 14, 15, have great similarity of expression to Eph. iv. 3, 4. ἐν τῷ συνδέσμῳ τῆς εἰρήνης. ἓν σῶμα καὶ ἓν πνεῦμα, καθὼς καὶ ἐκλήθητε ἐν μιᾷ ἐλπίδι τῆς κλήσεως ὑμῶν.

16. ὁ λόγος τοῦ Χριστοῦ. "The word of Christ," the uttered mind

Χριστοῦ ἐνοικείτω ἐν ὑμῖν πλουσίως, ἐν πάσῃ σοφίᾳ διδάσκοντες καὶ νουθετοῦντες ἑαυτούς, ψαλμοῖς ὕμνοις ᾠδαῖς πνευματικαῖς ἐν τῇ χάριτι ᾄδοντες ἐν τῇ καρδίᾳ
17 ὑμῶν τῷ θεῷ, καὶ πᾶν ὅ τι ἐὰν ποιῆτε ἐν λόγῳ ἢ ἐν ἔργῳ, πάντα ἐν ὀνόματι κυρίου Ἰησοῦ, εὐχαριστοῦντες τῷ θεῷ πατρὶ δι' αὐτοῦ.
18 Αἱ γυναῖκες, ὑποτάσσεσθε τοῖς ἀνδράσιν, ὡς ἀνῆκεν
19 ἐν κυρίῳ. οἱ ἄνδρες, ἀγαπᾶτε τὰς γυναῖκας καὶ μὴ
20 πικραίνεσθε πρὸς αὐτάς. Τὰ τέκνα, ὑπακούετε τοῖς γονεῦσιν κατὰ πάντα· τοῦτο γάρ ἐστιν εὐάρεστον ἐν

of Christ, nearly equivalent to "the inspiration of Christ."

It seems almost certain that the division of this sixteenth verse given in the English version is the right one. It is singular to find "psalms, hymns, and spiritual songs" represented as the media of instruction and admonition. But the parallel passage in Ephesians (v. 19, 20), λαλοῦντες ἑαυτοῖς ψαλμοῖς κ.τ.λ., makes it more than probable that this is what St. Paul meant. Divine inspiration will most naturally utter itself, we must suppose the Apostle to say, in adoration and thanksgiving: let these, rather than direct exhortations, be your modes of teaching and admonishing one another.

ἐν τῇ χάριτι, "with thankfulness." Compare 1 Cor. x. 30, εἰ ἐγὼ χάριτι μετέχω, τί βλασφημοῦμαι ὑπὲρ οὗ ἐγὼ εὐχαριστῶ;

17. With this comprehensive requirement compare, not only the parallel passage in Ephesians (v. 20), but the more exactly similar language in 1 St. Peter iv. 11, εἴ τις λαλεῖ, ὡς λόγια θεοῦ, εἴ τις διακονεῖ, ὡς ἐξ ἰσχύος ἧς χορηγεῖ ὁ θεός, ἵνα ἐν πᾶσιν δοξάζηται ὁ θεὸς διὰ Ἰησοῦ Χριστοῦ, (in which the reference is not only to sacerdotal speaking and ministering, but to all speaking and serving whatsoever;) and also 1 Cor. x. 31, εἴτε οὖν ἐσθίετε εἴτε πίνετε εἴτε τι ποιεῖτε, πάντα εἰς δόξαν θεοῦ ποιεῖτε.

18. ὡς ἀνῆκεν ἐν κυρίῳ. The mutual relations of the family and household belong to a Divine order, and are to be fulfilled in accordance with that order.

19. μὴ πικραίνεσθε, "do not indulge ill-temper towards them."

20. κατὰ πάντα. Compare ἐν παντί, Eph. v. 24. The obedience is to be general and comprehensive, not qualified by such exceptions as those by which the Pharisees "made the commandment of none effect" (St. Matthew xv. 3—6). But the duty of complete obedience may be crossed by other

21 κυρίῳ. οἱ πατέρες, μὴ ἐρεθίζετε τὰ τέκνα ὑμῶν, ἵνα
22 μὴ ἀθυμῶσιν. Οἱ δοῦλοι, ὑπακούετε κατὰ πάντα τοῖς κατὰ σάρκα κυρίοις, μὴ ἐν ὀφθαλμοδουλείαις ὡς ἀνθρωπάρεσκοι, ἀλλ᾽ ἐν ἁπλότητι καρδίας φοβούμενοι
23 τὸν κύριον. ὃ ἐὰν ποιῆτε, ἐκ ψυχῆς ἐργάζεσθε ὡς
24 τῷ κυρίῳ καὶ οὐκ ἀνθρώποις, εἰδότες ὅτι ἀπὸ κυρίου ἀπολήμψεσθε τὴν ἀνταπόδοσιν τῆς κληρονομίας. τῷ
25 κυρίῳ Χριστῷ δουλεύετε· ὁ γὰρ ἀδικῶν κομίσεται ὃ
V. 1 ἠδίκησεν, καὶ οὐκ ἔστιν προσωπολημψία. οἱ κύριοι, τὸ δίκαιον καὶ τὴν ἰσότητα τοῖς δούλοις παρέχεσθε, εἰδότες ὅτι καὶ ὑμεῖς ἔχετε κύριον ἐν οὐρανῷ.
2 Τῇ προσευχῇ προσκαρτερεῖτε γρηγοροῦντες ἐν αὐτῇ
3 ἐν εὐχαριστίᾳ, προσευχόμενοι ἅμα καὶ περὶ ἡμῶν, ἵνα ὁ θεὸς ἀνοίξῃ ἡμῖν θύραν τοῦ λόγου λαλῆσαι τὸ
4 μυστήριον τοῦ Χριστοῦ, δι᾽ ὃ καὶ δέδεμαι, ἵνα φανε-

duties if the parents do not command reasonably.

21. The *immediate* effect of an irritating use of parental authority would be to arouse resentment; but in the end the effect of such treatment, as St. Paul well teaches, must be to break the spirit and produce a servile temper.

24. τῆς κληρονομίας, "the inheritance" promised to all God's children. "Ye shall receive the requital of the inheritance," *i.e.* "the inheritance as a requital."

τῷ κυρίῳ Χριστῷ δουλεύετε, "ye are bond-servants to the Lord Christ." γάρ being omitted on the authority of the better MSS., there is a doubt whether δουλεύετε is in the indicative or the imperative. The next clause, ὁ γὰρ ἀδικῶν, κ.τ.λ. would follow better upon an imperative sense of δουλεύετε. But on the whole the sense "ye serve" appears to agree better with the context; the punctuation of the received text being retained. "Do your service as to the Lord; the Lord whom you serve is Christ. For he that does a wrong shall receive for the wrong he has done." In the parallel passage in Ephesians (vi. 8), doing *good* stands in the place of doing wrong.

25. προσωπολημψία. See note on Eph. vi. 9.

IV. 1. τὴν ἰσότητα, "fairness," —either actual *equality* as between one slave and another, or, more generally, that treatment which is commonly called "equal," equitable treatment.

3. θύραν τοῦ λόγου, "a door of the word," *i.e.* of the word in the

5 ῥώσω αὐτὸ ὡς δεῖ με λαλῆσαι. Ἐν σοφίᾳ περιπατεῖτε
6 πρὸς τοὺς ἔξω, τὸν καιρὸν ἐξαγοραζόμενοι. ὁ λόγος
ὑμῶν πάντοτε ἐν χάριτι, ἅλατι ἠρτυμένος, εἰδέναι πῶς
δεῖ ὑμᾶς ἑνὶ ἑκάστῳ ἀποκρίνεσθαι.
7 Τὰ κατ' ἐμὲ πάντα γνωρίσει ὑμῖν Τύχικος ὁ ἀγαπητὸς ἀδελφὸς καὶ πιστὸς διάκονος καὶ σύνδουλος ἐν
8 κυρίῳ, ὃν ἔπεμψα πρὸς ὑμᾶς εἰς αὐτὸ τοῦτο ἵνα γνῷ
9 τὰ περὶ ὑμῶν καὶ παρακαλέσῃ τὰς καρδίας ὑμῶν, σὺν
Ὀνησίμῳ τῷ πιστῷ καὶ ἀγαπητῷ ἀδελφῷ, ὅς ἐστιν ἐξ
ὑμῶν· πάντα ὑμῖν γνωριοῦσιν τὰ ὧδε.
10 Ἀσπάζεται ὑμᾶς Ἀρίσταρχος ὁ συναιχμάλωτός μου,

sense of the Gospel. Compare i. 25, 26, τὸν λόγον τοῦ θεοῦ, τὸ μυστήριον ... ἐφανερώθη.

5. τὸν καιρὸν ἐξαγοραζόμενοι. Here, as in Ephesians (v. 16), this remarkable phrase occurs in connexion with exhortations to careful and discreet behaviour. The Christians, being placed in circumstances of great difficulty and delicacy, needed to watch for the fit times of action, to "buy up the right moment."

6. It is again interesting to observe the likeness and the differences between this verse and its parallel in Ephesians (iv. 29). Speech "seasoned with salt" is opposed to λόγος σαπρός. Salt is the purifying and preserving principle, and speech thus seasoned answers to that which is "good for edification." "To know how you ought to answer each several person," is to know how you may do him the most good (ἵνα δῷ χάριν). The word χάρις, which has so many shades of meaning, appears not to be used in exactly the same sense in the two passages. In Ephesians, δοῦναι χάριν appears to be "to impart a benefit." Here ἐν χάριτι is "with grace," or, as we might say, "gracious." Kindness, not that of mere good nature, but that of a thoughtful and spiritual disposition, is expressed by χάρις.

7, 8. So in Eph. vi. 21, 22.

διάκονος, "a helper," as in that passage.

9. σὺν Ὀνησίμῳ. See the whole letter of St. Paul to Philemon. It is implied in that letter by the mention of Archippus, (compare Philemon 2 with Col. iv. 17,) that Philemon, and therefore Onesimus, belonged to Colossae.

10. Aristarchus, a Macedonian of Thessalonica, had been a companion of St. Paul for some time. He is at Ephesus at the time of the great tumult there (Acts xix. 29), travels with St. Paul from

καὶ Μάρκος ὁ ἀνεψιὸς Βαρνάβα, περὶ οὗ ἐλάβετε ἐν-
11 τολάς, (ἐὰν ἔλθῃ πρὸς ὑμᾶς, δέξασθε αὐτὸν), καὶ Ἰησοῦς
ὁ λεγόμενος Ἰοῦστος, οἱ ὄντες ἐκ περιτομῆς· οὗτοι
μόνοι συνεργοὶ εἰς τὴν βασιλείαν τοῦ θεοῦ, οἵτινες
12 ἐγενήθησάν μοι παρηγορία. ἀσπάζεται ὑμᾶς Ἐπαφρᾶς ὁ ἐξ ὑμῶν, δοῦλος Χριστοῦ Ἰησοῦ, πάντοτε
ἀγωνιζόμενος ὑπὲρ ὑμῶν ἐν ταῖς προσευχαῖς, ἵνα στῆτε
τέλειοι καὶ πεπληροφορημένοι ἐν παντὶ θελήματι τοῦ

Greece to Jerusalem (Acts xx. 4), and is with him on the voyage from Cæsarea to Italy (Acts xxvii. 2). He is now sharing St. Paul's imprisonment at Rome.

Μάρκος. The naming of Mark (here and in Philemon 24, see also 2 Tim. iv. 11) as a companion of St. Paul has the peculiar interest of proving that the breach described in Acts xiii. 13 and xv. 36—40, had not been a permanent one. John, who had once departed from Paul and Barnabas, and Barnabas with whom Paul had so sharp a contention because he wished afterwards to have his kinsman John with him that a temporary separation was the result, are now mentioned in terms of friendship; and "John surnamed Mark" appears to be an object of St. Paul's special solicitude.

11. If the clause οἱ ὄντες . . . τοῦ θεοῦ be read (as it is by Lachmann) without any pause after περιτομῆς, the meaning will be, "who, alone of the circumcision, are my fellow-workers unto the kingdom of God." But I should prefer placing a comma after περιτομῆς, and taking οὗτοι μόνοι συνεργοί in apposition to the preceding names; " — who are of the circumcision, these only being my fellow-workers unto the kingdom of God, men who have been a comfort to me." With a colon after περιτομῆς, οὗτοι μόνοι συνεργοί will be, "these alone *are* my fellow-workers."

12. It seems probable that the anxiety of the good Epaphras on behalf of his friends, and his report to St. Paul both of the Christian virtues of the Colossian Christians and of the dangers to which they were exposed, had much to do with the writing of this Epistle.

ἐν παντὶ θελήματι τοῦ θεοῦ, "in all God's will." The more regular rendering would be "in every will of God;" but the usage of θέλημα, corresponding to that of "will," makes the former rendering the more eligible.

13 θεοῦ. μαρτυρῶ γὰρ αὐτῷ ὅτι ἔχει πολὺν πόνον ὑπὲρ ὑμῶν καὶ τῶν ἐν Λαοδικείᾳ καὶ τῶν ἐν Ἱεραπόλει. 14 ἀσπάζεται ὑμᾶς Λουκᾶς ὁ ἰατρὸς ὁ ἀγαπητὸς καὶ 15 Δημᾶς. ἀσπάσασθε τοὺς ἐν Λαοδικείᾳ ἀδελφοὺς καὶ 16 Νυμφᾶν καὶ τὴν κατ' οἶκον αὐτοῦ ἐκκλησίαν. καὶ ὅταν ἀναγνωσθῇ παρ' ὑμῖν ἡ ἐπιστολή, ποιήσατε ἵνα καὶ ἐν τῇ Λαοδικέων ἐκκλησίᾳ ἀναγνωσθῇ, καὶ τὴν 17 ἐκ Λαοδικείας ἵνα καὶ ὑμεῖς ἀναγνῶτε. καὶ εἴπατε Ἀρχίππῳ Βλέπε τὴν διακονίαν ἣν παρέλαβες ἐν κυρίῳ, ἵνα αὐτὴν πληροῖς.
18 Ὁ ἀσπασμὸς τῇ ἐμῇ χειρὶ Παύλου. μνημονεύετέ μου τῶν δεσμῶν. ἡ χάρις μεθ' ὑμῶν.

13. πολὺν πόνον. Probably to be explained by reference to ἀγωνιζόμενος in the preceding verse: "much labouring of mind." Compare ii. 1.

14. Λουκᾶς καὶ Δημᾶς. Both are named again in Phil. 24. In 2 Tim. iv. 10, 11, Demas is said to have forsaken St. Paul, Luke to be still with him.

15. Lachmann reads, with some MS. authorities, "Nympha and the church in *her* house."

16. Laodicea, Hierapolis, and Colossæ were within a few miles of each other. Attempts have been made to identify the letter to the Laodiceans with that to Philemon or with that to the Ephesians. These attempts have no doubt been prompted by the hypothesis that no Epistles were written by St. Paul except those which have been preserved. But this is a most untenable theory. The greater probability is that a very large number of letters were written by him upon whom came daily the care of all the Churches. And it is most reasonable to assume that the letter referred to was one of those which have not been preserved.

17. It may fairly be assumed that the διακονία to which Archippus was to take heed was the office of superintending the Church at Colossæ. Compare Phil. 2.

18. The only part written by St. Paul, the rest of the Letter being dictated by him.

It is remarkable to observe how frequently St. Paul refers to his imprisonment as giving him a kind of authority, or a better right to be heard, amongst his fellow-believers. Compare, amongst many other passages, Philip. i. 12—14. Here, the only appeal made in his own handwriting is "Remember my bonds."

TO THE COLOSSIANS.

PAUL an Apostle of Christ Jesus by the will of God, and Timotheus the brother, to the holy and faithful brethren in Christ at Colossæ. Grace be to you and peace from God our Father.

We give thanks to God the Father of our Lord Jesus Christ always in prayers on your behalf, having heard of your faith in Christ Jesus and the love which you have towards all the saints, on account of the hope laid up for you in the heavens, of which you heard before in the word of truth of the Gospel, which has come amongst you, as also in all the world it is bearing fruit and increasing even as it does amongst you, from the day you heard it and came to know the grace of God in truth, even as you learnt it from Epaphras our beloved fellow-servant, who is a faithful minister of Christ on your behalf, who also made known to us your love in the spirit. On this account we also, since the day we heard of it, do not cease to pray for you and to ask that you may have the full knowledge of his will in all wisdom and spiritual understanding, so that you may walk worthily of the Lord unto all acceptableness, in every good work bearing fruit and increasing in the know-

11 ledge of God, strengthened with all power according to the might of his glory unto all patience and long-
12 suffering, with joy giving thanks to the Father who has enabled us to take our portion of the inheritance
13 of the saints in the light, who has delivered us from the power of darkness and transferred us into the
14 kingdom of the Son of his love, in whom we have our
15 redemption, the remission of our sins,—who is the image of the invisible God, firstborn of all creation,
16 inasmuch as in him were created all things in the heavens and on the earth, things visible and invisible, whether thrones or dominions or principalities or powers, all things have been created through him
17 and unto him, and he is before all, and all things
18 are held together in him, and he is the head of the body, the Church,—who is the beginning, the firstborn from the dead, that he in all things might have
19 priority, inasmuch as in him all the Fulness was
20 pleased to dwell, and by him to reconcile all things unto himself, having made peace through the blood of his cross, by him, whether things on earth or things
21 in the heavens; and you who were once alienated and enemies in mind in wicked works, now he has re-
22 conciled in the body of his flesh through his death, to present you holy and blameless and without re-
23 proach before him, if you abide in the faith grounded and settled and not moved away from the hope of the Gospel which you heard, which has been preached in all the creation under heaven, of which I Paul was made a minister.

24 Who now rejoice in my sufferings on your behalf, and fill up in my turn that which was lacking of the

afflictions of Christ in my flesh on behalf of his body, which is the Church, of which I was made a minister according to the dispensation of God given to me towards you, to fulfil the word of God, the mystery which from the ages and from the generations has been hidden, but now has been made manifest to his saints, to whom God has willed to make known what is the riches of the glory of this mystery among the Gentiles, which is Christ in you, the hope of glory, whom we proclaim instructing every man and teaching every man in all wisdom, that we may present every man perfect in Christ; unto which also I labour striving according to his energy which works in me with power.

For I wish you to know, what a conflict I have on your behalf, and for them at Laodicea, and for all who have not seen my face in the flesh, that they may be comforted in their hearts, being knit together in love and unto all the riches of the fulness of understanding, unto the knowledge of the mystery of God, even Christ, in whom are all the treasures of wisdom and knowledge hidden. This I say, that no one may mislead you with plausible words. For if in the flesh I am absent, yet in the spirit I am with you, rejoicing and beholding your order and the firm foundation of your faith in Christ. As therefore you have received Christ Jesus the Lord, walk in him, rooted and being built up in him, and becoming established in [the] faith as you have been taught, abounding in it with thanksgiving. Beware lest there shall be any one who shall make a prey of you through philosophy and vain deceit, according to the tradition of men, according to

II. 8 the rudiments of the world, and not according to Christ;
9 because in him dwells all the fulness of the Godhead
10 bodily, and you are in him fulfilled, who is the head
11 of all principality and power, in whom also you have been circumcised with a circumcision not done by hands, in the stripping off of the body of the flesh
12 in the circumcision of Christ, having been buried with him in your baptism, in which also you were raised with him through the faith of the working of God
13 who raised him from the dead. And you being dead in your trespasses and the uncircumcision of your flesh, he has made alive with him, having forgiven
14 us all our trespasses, wiping out the handwriting against us in decrees, which was contrary to us, and has taken it out of the midst, nailing it to the cross;
15 having stripped off principalities and powers he made a show of them confidently, triumphing over them in him.

16 Let no one therefore judge you in eating or in drinking, or in respect of feast or new moon or
17 sabbath, which are the shadow of future things, but
18 the body is that of Christ. Let no one take your prize from you at his will by preaching humility and the veneration of angels, going into things which he has not seen, vainly puffed up by the mind of
19 his flesh, and not holding fast the Head, from whom all the body being through the joints and ligaments supplied and knit together grows with the growth of
20 God. If you have died with Christ from the rudiments of the world, why, as if you were living in
21 the world, have you rules laid down for you, "Handle
22 not, taste not, touch not," (things which are all

meant to perish in using,) according to the prescriptions and teachings of men?—Which rules have indeed a show of wisdom in voluntary religion and humility and unsparing usage of the body, but are not of any value to the satisfying of the flesh.

If then you have risen together with Christ, seek the things above, where Christ is sitting at the right hand of God; mind things above, not things on the earth. For you have died, and your life is hidden with Christ in God: when Christ shall be manifested, who is our life, then shall you also with him be manifested in glory.

Mortify therefore your members which are upon the earth, fornication, uncleanness, passion, evil desire, and covetousness, which is idolatry, on account of which the anger of God comes upon the children of disobedience. In which things you also walked once, when you lived in them. But now, you also, put off all these things, anger, wrath, malice, evil speaking, filthy language out of your mouth; lie not one to another, having put off the old man with his deeds, and having put on the new man, which is being renewed unto knowledge after the image of him that created him, where there is not Greek and Jew, circumcision and uncircumcision, barbarian, Scythian, bond and free, but Christ is all things and in all. Put on therefore, as God's chosen saints and loved ones, a heart of pity, kindness, humility, meekness, longsuffering, bearing from one another and forgiving one another if any have a complaint against any, even as Christ has forgiven you, so do you; and in addition to all these put on love, which is the bond of perfect-

III. 15 ness. And let the peace of Christ rule in your hearts, unto which you have also been called in one body;
16 and be thankful. Let the word of Christ dwell in you richly in all wisdom, teaching and admonishing one another in psalms and hymns and spiritual songs,
17 with gratitude singing in your hearts to God. And whatsoever you do in word or in deed, do all in the name of the Lord Jesus, giving thanks to God the Father through him.
18 Wives, be subject to your husbands, as is becoming
19 in the Lord. Husbands, love your wives, and be not
20 irritable towards them. Children, obey your parents in all things: for this is well-pleasing in the Lord.
21 Fathers, provoke not your children, lest they be dis-
22 couraged. Bond-servants, obey in all things your masters according to the flesh, not with eye-service as men-pleasers, but in singleness of heart fearing
23 the Lord. Whatsoever you do, work from the heart
24 as to the Lord and not to men, knowing that from the Lord you shall receive the recompense of the in-
25 heritance; the Lord whom you serve is Christ. For he that does a wrong shall receive what he has done wrong, and there is no respect of the person.
IV. 1 Masters, afford to your bond-servants justice and equality, knowing that you also have a Master in heaven.
2 Persevere in prayer, watching in it with thanks-
3 giving, praying at the same time for us also, that God may open to us a door of the word, to speak the mystery of Christ, for the sake of which I am also
4 bound, that I may make it manifest as I ought to
5 speak. Walk in wisdom towards them that are with-

out, buying up the right time. Let your speech be IV. 6 always with grace, seasoned with salt, to know how you ought to answer every one.

All about me Tychicus will make known to you, 7 who is a beloved brother and faithful minister and fellow-servant in the Lord, whom I have sent unto 8 you for this very purpose, that he may know about you and may comfort your hearts; with Onesimus, 9 the faithful and beloved brother, who is of you. They will inform you of everything here.

Aristarchus my fellow-prisoner salutes you, and 10 Marcus cousin to Barnabas, concerning whom you have received injunctions, (if he come to you, receive him,) and Jesus called Justus, who are of the circum- 11 cision, these alone being fellow-workers unto the kingdom of God, who have been a comfort to me. Epaphras 12 your fellow-townsman salutes you, a servant of Christ Jesus, always striving in your behalf in prayers, that you may stand perfect and fulfilled in all God's will. For I bear him witness that he has much labour for 13 you and those at Laodicea and those at Hierapolis. Luke the beloved physician and Demas greet you. 14 Greet the brethren at Laodicea and Nymphas and 15 the church in his house. And when this letter has 16 been read amongst you, cause that it also be read in the Church of the Laodiceans and that you also read that from Laodicea. And say to Archippus, Look to 17 the ministry which thou hast received in the Lord, that thou fulfil it.

The salutation of me Paul with my own hand. 18 Remember my bonds. Grace be with you.

INTRODUCTION TO THE EPISTLE TO PHILEMON.

The chief interest of the short Letter to Philemon is in the light it throws on the social operation of the Gospel. The word preached by the Apostles, whilst it was unfolding the various relations which constitute Christian theology, was also working rapidly towards a social revolution through its personal and domestic influences. The Epistles to the Ephesians and the Colossians contain exhortations addressed both to masters and to slaves. Here in the Epistle to Philemon we have a living picture of the Gospel actually at work upon the institution of slavery. The picture includes the figures of Philemon the master, Onesimus the slave, and Paul the spiritual father of both. If we perceive in Ephesians some resemblance to a *hymn*, we may see in Philemon an *idyll* of the progress of Christianity.

The Epistle to Philemon was evidently written at the same time and sent by the same messenger as the Epistle to the Colossians. Philemon was a Christian of Colossæ, and the head of a considerable household, which may have included many slaves. He had received the Gospel either directly from the mouth of Paul himself, or by such a channel that he might virtually attribute his conversion to the Apostle (verse 19). Onesimus was a slave of his who had deserted him and made his way to Rome. There he was brought into contact with St. Paul, and became a believer in Christ. It seems probable that he was a person of spirit, not corrupted by the baseness natural to the servile condition, and that he had rebelled against the restraints of slavery. Such a person was more likely to yield to the trying demand now made on him by the Apostle. His father in Christ bade him go back again and surrender himself to his master; and Onesimus, whatever struggles it may have cost him, was prepared to obey. The Apostle, having gained this submission from the slave, feels that he may count upon a corresponding advance from the master. He begs him to receive Onesimus no longer as a slave, but as a beloved brother, or fellow-Christian.

We do not feel, as readers of the Epistle, any doubt that Philemon would act according to the Apostle's wish Apart from his sense of what he owed to Christ and to St. Paul, he would be greatly moved by such an act as his slave's voluntary return to him. But St. Paul pleads earnestly with him, acknowledging that he had been wronged by the desertion of his slave, and making the kindness for which he asked altogether an act of favour on Philemon's part. And he appeals to the claims which he, the veteran Apostle, the sufferer, the prisoner, had on the allegiance of Philemon, with that tender personal exactingness which would have been egotism if it had not been guarded by such pure disinterestedness.

The history of the work of Christianity in suppressing slavery could not have been begun more nobly than by this proof that the new relations created by the Gospel were incompatible with the natural relations of slavery, and that, if slaves were taught by the Christian doctrine to submit to the law of the land without murmuring, masters were taught to acknowledge themselves as bound by a higher law which would compel them to renounce the legal rights of owners of their fellow-men.

ΠΡΟΣ ΦΙΛΗΜΟΝΑ.

1 Παῦλος δέσμιος Χριστοῦ Ἰησοῦ καὶ Τιμόθεος ὁ
2 ἀδελφὸς Φιλήμονι τῷ ἀγαπητῷ καὶ συνεργῷ ἡμῶν καὶ
Ἀπφίᾳ τῇ ἀγαπητῇ καὶ Ἀρχίππῳ τῷ συνστρατιώτῃ
3 ἡμῶν καὶ τῇ κατ' οἶκόν σου ἐκκλησίᾳ. χάρις ὑμῖν
καὶ εἰρήνη ἀπὸ θεοῦ πατρὸς ἡμῶν καὶ κυρίου Ἰησοῦ
Χριστοῦ.

4 Εὐχαριστῶ τῷ θεῷ μου πάντοτε μνείαν σου ποιού-
5 μενος ἐπὶ τῶν προσευχῶν μου, ἀκούων σου τὴν ἀγάπην καὶ τὴν πίστιν ἣν ἔχεις πρὸς τὸν κύριον Ἰησοῦν

1. Φιλήμονι. Nothing is known of Philemon beyond what may be gathered from this Letter. See the Introduction.

2. τῇ ἀγαπητῇ. Another reading of high authority, preferred by Lachmann, is τῇ ἀδελφῇ.

Ἀρχίππῳ τῷ συνστρατιώτῃ. Mentioned in Col. iv. 17: "And say to Archippus, Take heed unto the ministry which thou hast received in the Lord, that thou fulfil it." The title "fellow-soldier" is given to Epaphroditus in Philip. ii. 25. The warfare implied is no doubt active warfare in the cause of the Gospel.

τῇ κατ' οἶκόν σου ἐκκλησίᾳ. As in Rom. xvi. 5, where the Church in the house of Aquila and Priscilla is mentioned. The phrase is purposely indefinite, and would include all believers who were in any way attached to the household. Archippus seems to have been a member of Philemon's household, whether as a near relation or in some other connexion, we have no means of knowing.

4. The Apostle's thanksgivings and prayers are blended together in his phrase as well as in reality.

5. It is possible that only the "love," and not the "faith," is to be considered as referring to "all the saints." But we may under-

6 καὶ εἰς πάντας τοὺς ἁγίους, ὅπως ἡ κοινωνία τῆς πιστεώς σου ἐνεργὴς γένηται ἐν ἐπιγνώσει παντὸς ἀγαθοῦ
7 τοῦ ἐν ἡμῖν εἰς Χριστὸν Ἰησοῦν. χάριν γὰρ ἔχομεν
πολλὴν καὶ παράκλησιν ἐπὶ τῇ ἀγάπῃ σου, ὅτι τά
σπλάγχνα τῶν ἁγίων ἀναπέπαυται διὰ σοῦ, ἀδελφέ.
8 Διὸ πολλὴν ἐν Χριστῷ παρρησίαν ἔχων ἐπιτάσσειν
9 σοι τὸ ἀνῆκον, διὰ τὴν ἀγάπην μᾶλλον παρακαλῶ.
τοιοῦτος ὢν ὡς Παῦλος πρεσβύτης, νυνὶ δὲ καὶ δέσμιος

stand "faith towards all the saints," in the light of the phrase which follows, ἡ κοινωνία τῆς πιστεώς σου, as meaning a readiness to acknowledge *the community* of faith with all other believers.

6. This is the purport of the Apostle's prayer. It is somewhat obscurely expressed. The uncertainty arises in part out of what is a frequent cause of ambiguity in St. Paul's language, his use of the first person plural. It is not impossible that ἐν ἡμῖν here means "in me." The Apostle's desire is that Philemon may feel entirely with him as to what is "good" in the matter about which he writes. He himself loved Onesimus, and rejoiced to own him as a brother in Christ. He had been commending the sense of brotherhood shewn by Philemon towards his fellow-believers. A common Christian consciousness will manifest its activity in a common appreciation of the same things as good. St. Paul prays, therefore, that Philemon's fellow-feeling as a Christian may be operative in the recognition of every good thing which there was in Paul himself. The same sense may be retained in a more generalized form, if we take ἐν ἡμῖν to refer to Christians in general. Other interpretations seem to leave the words ἐν ἐπιγνώσει παντὸς ἀγαθοῦ τοῦ ἐν ἡμῖν rather pointless. Compare the phrases τὸ ἀγαθόν σου (verse 14) and εἰ οὖν με ἔχεις κοινωνόν (verse 17). Was Christian brotherhood to be a real power of goodness or not? was the question St. Paul was putting. εἰς Χριστὸν Ἰησοῦν. Christ is named as the end to which all such activity of the common Christian consciousness should have reference.

7. Χάριν γὰρ ἔχομεν πολλήν. We need not hesitate to adopt the easier reading, χαρὰν γὰρ πολλὴν ἔσχον, which is found in almost all the more important MSS.

9. τοιοῦτος ὢν ὡς Παῦλος, "such a one as Paul is," namely, an elder, and now a prisoner. It seems better to place a comma, as Lachmann does, after Παῦλος. The Apostle lays great stress, as he does so often, upon the sufferings of his imprisonment as giving him

10 Χριστοῦ Ἰησοῦ, παρακαλῶ σε περὶ τοῦ ἐμοῦ τέκνου,
11 ὃν ἐγέννησα ἐν τοῖς δεσμοῖς, Ὀνήσιμον, τόν ποτέ σοι ἄχρηστον, νυνὶ δὲ σοὶ καὶ ἐμοὶ εὔχρηστον, ὃν ἀνέ-
12 πεμψα. σὺ δὲ αὐτόν, τοῦτ' ἔστιν τὰ ἐμὰ σπλάγχνα,
13 ὃν ἐγὼ ἐβουλόμην πρὸς ἐμαυτὸν κατέχειν, ἵνα ὑπὲρ σοῦ
14 μοι διακονῇ ἐν τοῖς δεσμοῖς τοῦ εὐαγγελίου, χωρὶς δὲ τῆς σῆς γνώμης οὐδὲν ἠθέλησα ποιῆσαι, ἵνα μὴ ὡς κατὰ ἀνάγκην τὸ ἀγαθόν σου ᾖ ἀλλὰ κατὰ ἑκούσιον·
15 τάχα γὰρ διὰ τοῦτο ἐχωρίσθη πρὸς ὥραν ἵνα αἰώνιον
16 αὐτὸν ἀπέχῃς, οὐκ ἔτι ὡς δοῦλον ἀλλ' ὑπὲρ δοῦλον, ἀδελφὸν ἀγαπητόν, μάλιστα ἐμοί, πόσῳ δὲ μᾶλλον σοὶ
17 καὶ ἐν σαρκὶ καὶ ἐν κυρίῳ· εἰ οὖν με ἔχεις κοινωνόν,
18 προσλαβοῦ αὐτὸν ὡς ἐμέ. εἰ δέ τι ἠδίκησέν σε ἢ

a title to be heard with the more respect and affection.

10. Ὀνήσιμον. This word, meaning "profitable" or "useful," was probably a common slave's name. Its signification is referred to in the words which follow, ἄχρηστον, εὔχρηστον.

12. σὺ δὲ αὐτόν. The word προσλαβοῦ after these is omitted by Tischendorf; but it has considerable MS. authority in its favour, and we are obliged to supply some such word in translation. Lachmann omits σὺ δέ also, reading ὃν ἀνέπεμψά σοι, αὐτόν, τουτέστιν τὰ ἐμὰ σπλάγχνα.

13. The *nature* of the "ministry" implied in the words διάκονος and διακονεῖν is often somewhat doubtful. We may take it here as including whatever help could be rendered to St. Paul, remembering that all his occupation and interest lay in preaching the Gospel.

14. τὸ ἀγαθόν. Compare this with παντὸς ἀγαθοῦ in verse 6. If St. Paul had retained Onesimus, presuming on Philemon's willingness to give up his claim to his services, the goodness, or good act, would have been this sacrifice, rendered without choice being given him. As Onesimus was returning to his master, Philemon's goodness must take another form, that of forgiving Onesimus and treating him as a brother. For it does not appear that St. Paul wished Philemon to part with Onesimus. See the next verse, ἵνα αἰώνιον αὐτὸν ἀπέχῃς.

15. The running away of Onesimus may have been *permitted*, with a view to its being overruled for good.

19 ὀφείλει, τοῦτο ἐμοὶ ἐλλόγα. ἐγὼ Παῦλος ἔγραψα τῇ ἐμῇ χειρί, ἐγὼ ἀποτίσω· ἵνα μὴ λέγω σοι ὅτι καὶ
20 σεαυτόν μοι προσοφείλεις. ναί, ἀδελφέ, ἐγώ σου ὀναίμην ἐν κυρίῳ· ἀνάπαυσόν μου τὰ σπλάγχνα ἐν Χριστῷ.
21 Πεποιθὼς τῇ ὑπακοῇ σου ἔγραψά σοι, εἰδὼς ὅτι καὶ
22 ὑπὲρ ὃ λέγω ποιήσεις. ἅμα δὲ καὶ ἑτοίμαζέ μοι ξενίαν· ἐλπίζω γὰρ ὅτι διὰ τῶν προσευχῶν ὑμῶν χαρισθήσομαι ὑμῖν.
23 Ἀσπάζεταί σε Ἐπαφρᾶς ὁ συναιχμάλωτός μου ἐν
24 Χριστῷ Ἰησοῦ, Μάρκος, Ἀρίσταρχος, Δημᾶς, Λουκᾶς, οἱ συνεργοί μου.
25 Ἡ χάρις τοῦ κυρίου ἡμῶν Ἰησοῦ Χριστοῦ μετὰ τοῦ πνεύματος ὑμῶν.

19. It is possible that St. Paul's *autograph* begins here, the previous part of the Epistle having been dictated; but this is doubtful.

σεαυτὸν προσοφείλεις. Philemon had apparently owed his conversion to St. Paul; but this may have taken place at Ephesus or elsewhere, and it is not necessary to assume that St. Paul had been at Colossæ.

20. ὀναίμην. The word is almost certainly suggested by the name Ὀνήσιμος.

22. It is not safe to infer from the hope expressed here, that it was realized. There was no infallibility attaching to St. Paul's anticipations. He had said to the Ephesians (Acts xx. 25), "I know that ye all, among whom I have gone preaching the kingdom of God, shall see my face no more."

Yet, if he went to Colossæ, he was sure to go to Ephesus also. And in 1 Tim. iv. 13, he says, "Till I come [to Ephesus], give attendance to reading, to exhortation, to doctrine."

23. Ἐπαφρᾶς. See Col. i. 7; iv. 12, 13. He must have been a personal friend of Philemon.

24. Μάρκος. Col. iv. 10; Acts xv. 37—39. Ἀρίσταρχος. Col. iv. 10; Acts xxvii. 2. Δημᾶς, Λουκᾶς. Col. iv. 14; 2 Tim. iv. 10, 11.

25. μετὰ τοῦ πνεύματος ὑμῶν. So at the end of the Epistle to the Galatians; and of the second to Timothy, except that σοῦ stands there instead of ὑμῶν. Here St. Paul is probably referring to the *household* of Philemon. He assumes, as in Gal., that there is *one* spirit of many members.

TO PHILEMON.

1 PAUL a prisoner of Christ Jesus and Timotheus the brother, to Philemon our beloved friend and fellow-worker, 2 and to Apphia the beloved, and to Archippus our fellow-soldier, and to the Church in thy house: 3 Grace be to you and peace from God our Father and our Lord Jesus Christ.

4 I thank my God, always making mention of thee in my prayers, 5 hearing of thy love and faith which thou hast towards the Lord Jesus and towards all the saints, 6 that the fellowship of thy faith may be made effectual in the acknowledging of every good thing in us unto Christ Jesus. 7 For I have had much joy and consolation in thy love, because the hearts of the saints have been refreshed by thee, brother. 8 Wherefore, having much confidence in Christ to *enjoin* thee what is becoming, 9 for love's sake I rather beseech thee; being such a one as Paul, an elder, and now also a prisoner of Christ Jesus, 10 I beseech thee concerning my own child, whom I have begotten in my bonds, Onesimus, 11 who was once useless to thee, but is now useful to thee and to me, 12 whom I have sent back; do thou receive him, that is, my own heart. 13 Whom I wished to retain with me, that in thy behalf he might minister to thee in the bonds of the Gospel:

14 but without thy mind I would not do anything, that thy goodness should not be as of necessity,
15 but willingly. For perhaps on this account he was separated for a time, that thou mightest receive him
16 for ever, no longer as a slave, but beyond a slave, a brother beloved, specially to me, but how much
17 more to thee both in the flesh and in the Lord. If then thou holdest me as a partner, receive him as
18 myself; and if he has injured thee or owes thee any-
19 thing, put it to my account. I Paul have written it with my own hand, I will repay it;—that I may not tell thee that thou owest even thyself to me. Yes,
20 brother, let me have profit of thee in the Lord; refresh my heart in Christ.
21 Trusting in thy obedience I have written to thee, knowing that thou wilt do even beyond what I say.
22 And at the same time prepare me a lodging; for I hope that through your prayers I shall be given to
23 you. There salute thee Epaphras my fellow-prisoner
24 in Christ Jesus, Marcus, Aristarchus, Demas, Lucas,
25 my fellow-workers. The grace of our Lord Jesus Christ be with your spirit.

ON THE TRACES OF FOREIGN ELEMENTS IN THE DOCTRINE OF THESE EPISTLES; AND ESPECIALLY ON THE GNOSTICAL TERMS OCCURRING IN THEM.

THERE are certain terms occurring in important passages of these Epistles, especially in that to the Colossians, which became prominent afterwards in the phraseology of the Gnostical systems of the second century. The presence of such terms in the New Testament has been made one of the strongest arguments for the later date and spurious composition of some of its books. It has been contended, especially by Baur and the school of Tübingen, that the books in which the Gnostical terms occur must be contemporaneous with the great Gnostical systems, and therefore cannot be the writings of St. Paul or St. John. It is a very arbitrary assertion that those terms could not have been used before the Gnostical theories were developed; but the questions raised by the occurrence of these terms are of great interest and importance. Was there a Gnostical element in the teaching of the Apostles? Were the Apostles protesting against rival systems of religion? Did the leading Gnostics appropriate to their own use language which properly belonged to the Apostles? What are we to say as to the phrases "the Pleroma or Fulness," "principalities and powers," "the prince of the power of the air," "the world-rulers of this darkness," "the image of the invisible God," "the first-born of all creation," which belong to Gnostical systems as much as to these Epistles?

Little as we know of the Church history of the latter half of the first century, we are not without materials for giving a general answer to such questions. It is true that the great and prolific development of matured Gnostical systems took place in the course of the second century. It may be admitted as very probable that no sect of Gnostics existed in Asia Minor at the time when we suppose St. Paul to have been writing to the Ephesians and the Colossians. But the *Gnosis* was not an original creed or philosophy. Some of its leading sects may well have arisen quite independently of one another. They took up elements already existing in the speculative traditions of the age, and combined them in various forms. Any one describing Gnosticism must say that it mixed some of the notions of Oriental theosophy with some of the tenets of the Christian Church. It belongs to its very essence to be composite. And when any one of the Gnostical systems is analysed, the largest portion of it will always be referred to more ancient mystical speculations. The only question will generally be, to which of the older theosophies it should be affiliated. The Zend Avesta, Buddhism, Hinduism, the religions of Egypt and of Phœnicia, the Græco-Judaism of Philo, all put in claims which are entitled to consideration.*

It is a most important fact for the early history of the Christian Faith, that in the age of Christ and of the Apostles there was a general intermingling, especially in Egypt, Syria, and Asia Minor, of almost all the speculations of the ancient world. This was brought about partly by the movements of the Jews, partly by the conquests of Alexander. The long Captivity of the Jews in Babylon, and the dispersion which continued after their return, had made them familiar with the Oriental ways of thinking concerning the invisible world. The expeditions of Alex-

* A very lucid analysis of Gnosticism may be found in the work of M. Matter, "Histoire du Gnosticisme."

ander had brought the West and the far East into contact. Alexandria, under his successors, became the point of confluence of all religions and all philosophies. The extension of the Roman empire still further increased the locomotion of old ideas. All the notions which had ever been systematized in the East may be said to have been floating loosely together in the intellectual heaven at the beginning of the Christian era. Almost anywhere a thinking and inquiring mind had access to some variety of Oriental lore.

Another fact which concerns us is, that Jews were more disposed than men of other nations to assimilate foreign religion and philosophy. From whatever cause, the most actively eclectic minds in those ages were Jewish minds. This is something of a paradox. For undoubtedly the Jews by their law and worship were in a peculiar degree separated from other nations. But the depth and the truth of their own faith appear to have given them an interest in whatever had laid hold strongly of the convictions of other races. The Jewish intellect was accordingly more fertile than any other in new theosophic combinations. The nascent Christian Church received all its influences of foreign thought through Jewish channels. Simon Magus, the earliest teacher to whom a Gnostical school referred itself, being a Samaritan, is hardly to be regarded as an exception. It is important, when we observe the mixture of Jewish with Oriental or Platonizing ideas implied in the Apostolical writings, to remember that all the rival teachers in the Church, whatever they taught, began with Judaism, and spoke to the believers in Christ as inheritors with them of the common Jewish traditions.

The principal terms or ideas in these Epistles which remind us of the subsequent Gnostical systems, and of which we are to seek illustrations in writings anterior to the age of St. Paul, may be stated as follows:—

1. The Pleroma, or Fulness. This word occurs as an

equivalent to the infinite Divine Nature, in Col. i. 19, "all the Fulness was pleased to dwell in him," and in Col. ii. 9, "In him dwells all the Fulness of the Godhead bodily." It is used to denote Divine perfection in Eph. iii. 19, "that ye may be filled unto all the fulness of God;" and in Eph. iv. 13, "until we all attain to the measure of stature of the fulness of Christ." In Eph. i. 23, the Church, the Body of Christ, is called "the Fulness of him who fills all things in all." As this last passage reminds us, cognate forms of the word "full" are frequent in these Epistles, and produce phrases which are at least embarrassing to translate, if the meaning of them is not also somewhat indefinite. It is evident that terms expressive of the idea of *fulness* were welcome to the writer's mind.

2. The Son, the Image of the invisible God, the First-born of all creation, the Head of the Universe, the ideal Man. It is a matter of surprise that the title of the Logos or Word does not occur in these Epistles. It would be a mistake, I imagine, to draw any inference from its absence, or to regard the non-occurrence of it otherwise than as an accident.

3. The Prince of the power of the air, and the power or kingdom of darkness (Eph. ii. 2; Col. i. 13).

4. The principalities and powers, good and evil (Eph. iii. 10, &c.); the world-rulers of this darkness.

5. The use of special religious and ascetical practices in order to rise from the earthly to the heavenly (Col. ii. 16—23).

These ideas, whether as adopted or rejected by St. Paul, would serve as points of contact between his teaching in these Epistles, and the various systems of Gnosticism which sprang up in the next century: but our present object is to see whether they are not equally to be found in books or traditions to which St. Paul and his contemporaries had access. The writings of the *Neo-Platonists* are therefore beyond our scope ; and, although in the opinion of some critics the distinctive speculations of the *Kabbalah* are to be traced back to a date before the coming of Christ, the books of the Kabbalah are themselves so much more modern, and its earlier traditions,—supposing them to exist independently,—are so similar to the doctrines of Philo and of the Zend Avesta, that we may conveniently put the Kabbalah also aside.

The lore which may really have influenced the mind of St. Paul is to be found in the Apocrypha, in Philo, and in the Zend Avesta.

Two books of the Apocrypha, " Ecclesiasticus " and the " Wisdom of Solomon," are remarkable for their doctrine concerning Wisdom. In the canonical book of Proverbs Wisdom is represented as speaking to men, and there is much praise of knowledge and understanding ; but the language used there is not to be identified with that of the two Apocryphal books. In these Wisdom is not merely personified, but treated as a second Divine person. What elsewhere would be the Divine *Word* is here the Divine Wisdom. Ecclesiasticus is the older book of the two, and is considered to be more exclusively Jewish. The Wisdom of Solomon bears marks of a later origin,—its date however being still anterior to the age of Philo,—and of being affected by Grecian thought. The following passages are from Ecclesiasticus xxiv. : " I [Wisdom] came out of the mouth of the Most High, and covered the earth as a cloud (v. 3)." "He created me from the beginning before the world, and I shall never fail. In the holy tabernacle I served before him : and so was I established in Sion. Likewise in the beloved city he gave me rest, and in Jerusalem was my power. And I took root in an honourable people, even in the portion of the Lord's inheritance" (vv. 9—12). " I am the mother of fair love, and fear, and knowledge, and holy hope : I therefore, being eternal, am given to all my children which are named of him" (v. 18). The style of the "Wisdom of Solomon" is more rhetorical and ornate, and its language is hardly to be taken as plain prose; but it exhibits an evidently increased tendency to regard Wisdom as a distinct Divine emanation. "Wisdom was with thee: which knoweth thy works, and was present when thou madest the world, and knew what was acceptable in thy sight, and right in thy commandments" (ix. 9). "For Wisdom, which is the worker of all things, taught me: for in her is an understanding spirit, holy, one only, manifold, subtil, lively, clear, undefiled, plain, not subject to hurt, loving the thing that is good, quick, which cannot be letted, ready to do good, kind to man, steadfast, sure, free from care, having all power, overseeing all things, and going through all understanding pure and most subtil spirits. For Wisdom is more moving than any motion: she passeth and goeth through all things by reason of her pureness. For she is the breath of the power of God, and a pure influence flowing from the glory of the Almighty: therefore can no defiled thing fall into her. For she is the brightness of the everlasting light, the unspotted mirror of the power of God, and the image of his goodness. And being but one, she can do all things: and remaining in herself, she maketh all things new: and in all ages entering into holy souls, she maketh men friends of God, and prophets" (vii. 22—27). The fine passage describing God's judgment in the destruction of the firstborn in Egypt shews that the writer of this book used the expression "the Word" rather in the manner of St. Paul than of the Targums or Philo or St. John. "For while all things were in quiet silence, and that night was in the midst of her swift course, thine Almighty word leaped down from heaven out of thy royal throne, as a fierce man of war into the midst of a land of destruction, and brought thine unfeigned commandment as a sharp sword, and standing up filled all things with death; and it touched the heaven, but it stood upon the earth" (xviii. 14—16).

With the Apocrypha we may connect such indications of the tendencies of Jewish thought as may be found in the Septuagint Version and in the paraphrases called the Targums.

The Septuagint shews traces of a repugnance to use expressions which speak of God as being in any way *visible*. The Hebrew text says that when Moses and Aaron, Nadab and Abihu, and seventy of the elders of Israel, went up, "they saw the God of Israel" (Ex. xxiv. 10); but the Greek Version has "they saw the place where the God of Israel stood:" and in the next verse, for "they saw God," "they were seen in the place of God" is substituted. In Numbers xii. 8, for "the similitude of the Lord shall he behold," the Septuagint has "he saw the glory of the Lord." In Isaiah xxxviii. 11, for "I shall not see the Lord, even the Lord, in the land of the living," we have in the Greek "I shall no longer see the salvation of God in the land of the living." The word "powers," δυνάμεις, which is a significant word both in Philo and in St. Paul, is the rendering of the LXX. for Sabaoth or *tsebaoth* in the phrase "the Lord of hosts." *Tsebaoth* means the army or fighting men of the children of Israel. But the Greek translators preferred to think of God as the Lord of the armies *of heaven*. In Gen. i. 27, we have another variation. The Hebrew has "male and female created he *them*." The Greek, "male and female created he *him*" (ἄρσεν καὶ θῆλυ ἐποίησεν αὐτόν), implying the creation of the ideal Man with a twofold nature.

The Targums are a kind of paraphrase in Chaldee or Aramaic of the Hebrew text of the Old Testament. After the Captivity the Hebrew had become an unfamiliar dialect to the Jews, and it was necessary to translate the Scriptures when they were read on the Sabbath days into the popular language. This was done orally by persons called *interpreters*, and for many generations it was strictly forbidden to write down and embody in a book the traditional explanatory version. About the end of the second century after Christ the Targum is said to have been first committed to writing; but what was then written had been handed down from earlier times. The Targum on the Pentateuch, called the Targum of Onkelos, embodies the earliest traditional version of the Hebrew text. In this Targum is observed " an aversion to anthropopathies and anthropomorphisms; in fact to any term which could in the eyes of the multitude lower the idea of the Highest Being. . . . a repugnance to bring the Divine Being into too close contact, as it were, with man. It erects a kind of reverential barrier, a sort of invisible medium of awful reverence, between the Creator and the creature." To this Targum belongs especially the use of the term "Memra," the Word or Logos, and also of "Shekinah," the holy presence or glory of God. Thus, for "The voice of the Lord God was heard" (Gen. iii. 8), the Targum has "The voice of the Word." For "He will dwell in the tents of Shem,"—"the Shekinah will dwell." For "the Lord went up from Abraham,"—"the glory of God went up." For "God came to Abimelech,"—"the Word from God came." [See Mr. Deutsch's Article on Targums in the Dictionary of the Bible.]

Philo. That peculiar form of Judaism, of which the Book of Wisdom is an early representative, found its home in Alexandria. A great number of Jews settled in Egypt, and there became thoroughly imbued with Greek philosophy and literature, without abandoning their ancient faith. Continuing to accept their sacred books as of Divine authority, they studied them through a Greek medium. A habit grew up of treating the Biblical narrative as allegory, and of attaching a more or less arbitrary spiritual significance to its names and incidents and phrases. The school of Grecian Judaism was fortunate enough to find a first-rate literary representative in Philo. Not an original philosopher himself, he had a very quick and fertile mind, and was eminently ingenious in maturing and expounding the method of interpretation which prevailed in his time at Alexandria. He was born about 20 B.C., and went on an embassy to the Emperor Caius Caligula in A.D. 40. His works consist chiefly of a series of commentaries on the books of Moses, his language being that of the Platonic school of his day. Philo becomes a most interesting study when considered as a contemporary of our Lord and of the Apostles. What we have for our present purpose to observe is that Philo evidently did not stand alone, but represented the Judaism of Egypt; that St. Paul must have had many opportunities of reading the works of Philo, and that the Alexandrian mode of interpreting Scripture could not possibly have escaped his knowledge. One of the Apostle's most powerful coadjutors at Ephesus and in Achaia was Apollos, "born at Alexandria, an eloquent man and mighty in the Scriptures" (Acts xviii. 24—28). It can hardly be an error therefore to assume in St. Paul an acquaintance with any doctrines which are to be found in Philo.

The passages which I proceed to quote are chiefly intended to illustrate the views then prevailing amongst an important section of the Jews as to the development of the Divine nature in Creation and in the government of the world. For those who desire to know more of Philo, his writings are not at all difficult to read and are easily accessible.

Upon the saying "the Lord came down to see the city and the tower," (Gen. xi. 5,) Philo observes that *motion* can only be predicated of God figuratively or in the way of accommodation. "But all things are filled by God, who embraces and is not embraced, to whom alone it belongs to be both everywhere and nowhere:—nowhere, because he has himself begotten both room and space together with material objects, and it is not legitimate to speak of that which made it as being embraced in anything that has been made; and everywhere, because having extended his powers through earth and water and air and heaven he has left no part of the world desert, but having drawn together all things through all he has bound them tight with invisible chains, that they should never be loosed." (De confusione linguarum, i. 426.) Similarly he says (i. 88), " God has filled all things and has gone through all, and has left nothing empty or desert of himself."

Concerning the Word of God, the language of Philo may be conveniently learnt from the various titles given under the heading *Verbum Divinum* in the index of the edition of Mangey. " The Divine Word, the ideal *locus* or place of the world, the idea of ideas, the image of God, the exemplar of light, God's elder, eldest, firstborn, Son, maker of the world, ruler of things, most ancient of all things, eternal, pillar and bond, seal of things, divider ($\tau o \mu \epsilon \acute{u} s$), mediator, chief pontiff of God, sees through all things, nourishment of souls, God of imperfect things, waters the virtues like a stream, fountain of delight, vicegerent of God, contains and fills all things, second God." The passage referred to under the word "divider" is one of the most curious. On the words "he divided them in the midst," (Gen. xv. 10,) Philo comments as follows: "Understand that God cuts the natures of bodies and things which seem most firmly united, by his Word, the cutter of all things,—which, sharpened to the finest edge, divides without ceasing all perceptible things; and when it has penetrated to the elements which are said to be indivisible and without parts, this cutter begins, from these, to divide the things contemplated in thought into unnamed and uncircumscribed portions, and 'cuts the leaves of gold into hairs,' (Exod. xxxix. 3,) as Moses says, length without breadth, like imaginary lines." Philo then mentions various divisions, as into light and heavy, rational and irrational, &c.; and concludes, "Thus God having sharpened his word the cutter of all things divides the shapeless and unqualified substance of things in general, and the four elements of the world which are separated out of it, and the animals and plants which are constituted of these." (Quis divinarum heres, i. 491.)

God sees all things by his own light. "For the Eye of absolute Being needs no other light in order to perceive, but being itself the archetypal brightness it sends out a thousand rays, none of them perceptible by sense, but all by intellect." (De Cherubim, i. 156.)

Moses having asked to be permitted to see God himself, is told that this is impossible. He acquiesces, but goes on to plead,—" But I entreat that I may behold at least the glory that surrounds thee; and thy glory I deem to be the powers which form thy body-guard, which not having yet perceived I earnestly desire to behold. God answered and said, The powers which thou seekest after are altogether invisible and to be apprehended by the understanding, as I am. I do not say that they are already being apprehended by the understanding, but that, if they could be apprehended, it would not be by sense, but by the purest intelligence. But being naturally inapprehensible in their essence they yet exhibit a kind of impress and likeness of their activity. Just as seals, when applied to wax or any similar material, stamp off any number of impressions, without losing any part of themselves, but remaining as they were, —so you must conceive of the powers which surround me as communicating qualities to things unqualified and forms to formless things, and neither changing nor losing anything of their eternal nature. Those among you who name them 'ideas' [*forms*] are not far from the mark, since they give form to all existing things, ordering things disordered, and imparting limits and definition and shape to things without boundaries, undefined, and shapeless, and generally altering the worse into the better. Do not hope therefore that you will ever be able to apprehend either me or any of my powers in essence. But things attainable, as I said, I readily and gladly communicate." (De monarchiâ, ii. 219.)

Angels are ministers of the All-ruler. "These are called by the other philosophers *dæmons*, but the sacred word is wont to call them angels [messengers], using a more appropriate name, because they convey the commands of the father to his offspring, and the wants of the offspring to their father; wherefore they are introduced as 'ascending and descending,' not because God who knows all beforehand needs messengers to inform him, but because it was expedient for us mortal creatures to have 'words' [a name for angels] as intervening mediators, on account of the dread and amazement with which the All-ruler and the mighty strength of his sovereignty would strike us.... For, not to say punishments, but even surpassing and untempered benefits would be more than we could bear, if he should himself put them forth to us by himself, without using others as his ministers." (De somniis, i. 642.)

There is a high strain in Philo's doctrine with regard to the ascent of the soul towards God. "The mind," he says, "when it purely worships God, is not human, but divine." (i. 485.) In the following passage he is explaining that the soul must "go out of itself" if it would inherit Divine things. The soul is represented as saying that it has "gone out," not only from the body and from sense or perception, but also from reason. "I removed from reason also, when I became aware of its great unreasonableness, although it lifted up and inflated itself. For it ventured on no trifling enterprise, to shew me objects by means of shadows, things by means of words, which was impracticable. Therefore it poured itself around unstable things, and babbled about them, being unable to set forth with distinct presentation the peculiarities of things by the community of names. But being taught by experience like a foolish child, I learnt that it was better to go out from all these, and to offer up the powers of each to God, who gives its bodily frame to the body, and causes the perception to perceive, and enables the reason to speak." The soul is then addressed: "In the same way in which thou hast gone out from those other things, withdraw and remove from thyself also. And what is this?—Do not deal out thought and reflection and apprehension to thyself, but carry these also and offer them up to him who enables thee to understand accurately, and to apprehend without mistake." (Quis rerum divinarum heres, i. 483.)

Faith, and Grace, are both made much of by Philo. There is a somewhat rhetorical eulogy of Faith in De Abrahamo, ii. 39, where it is called "the queen of virtues," "the only infallible and certain good, . . . the bettering in all things of the soul which has cast itself for support upon the Author of all things, who can do all, and who desires what is best." "The covenant is a symbol of *grace*, which God has set between himself who bestows and man who receives. This is a surpassing benefit, that nothing should intervene between God and the soul except *maiden grace*." (De mutatione nominum, i. 586.)

The Zoroastrian Religion.

It is a disputed question, whether the elements which Philo has blended with the doctrine of the Hebrew Scriptures were drawn exclusively from Grecian philosophy, or in part from Oriental traditions. On the one hand, it is quite conceivable that the mingling of the Platonic theory of ἰδέαι with the Jewish faith might have produced all that we find in Philo. But on the other hand, Philo, living and studying at Alexandria, can hardly have failed to be influenced by Eastern systems of theosophy; and the very faith which he inherited from his fathers had certainly been affected by its contact with one great Eastern religion, and that the one of which Philo's language most reminds us. This was the Zoroastrian, the religion of the Persians.

Before the termination of the Jewish Captivity, Babylon was conquered by Cyrus the Persian. This took place in the year 538 B.C. The return of the Jews began in the year 536 B.C. and was continued during the reign of Darius the son of Hystaspes, who came to the throne in B.C. 521. The favourable expressions in the book of Isaiah with regard to Cyrus (the Lord's shepherd, the Lord's anointed) are well known (xliv. 28, xlv. 1). The religion of the Persians, which had no worship of idols, was received with sympathy by the Jews, and exercised an undoubted influence upon the Jewish mind. Concurrently with other causes, it led to a greater development of liturgical prayer, and to a more definite belief in a heavenly hierarchy, including both good and evil angels.

The religion of Cyrus and Darius is known to have been the worship of Or-muzd, or Ahura-Mazda. The Inscriptions recently deciphered at Behistun and Persepolis bear abundant testimony to this fact. The worship of Or-muzd is called Zoroastrian, because its traditions name Zoroaster, or Zerduscht, or Zarathustra, as the teacher and legislator from whom it is derived. The Zoroastrian religion is peculiarly interesting because of its great antiquity, and because its ancient books are only now beginnning to be thoroughly known. The doctrinal resemblances of the Zoroastrian system to the language of St. Paul and St. John, as well as to the later Gnostical systems, make it especially important for the study of the development of Christian doctrine.

The ancient books of this system are contained in the

collection called the Zend Avesta. These are the only books now existing in the language called the Zend, which has been found by comparison to be a sister dialect to Sanskrit. The books have been preserved in the hands of the Parsees in India, the modern remnant of the Zoroastrians, and were brought to Europe towards the close of the last century by M. Anquetil du Perron. The aids for deciphering and interpreting the Zend MSS. have been a Sanskrit version (Neriosengh's), a more ancient version into a language called Pehlevi, and the traditional renderings of the Parsees. M. Anquetil made an imperfect translation into French by means of Parsee assistance in Bombay; but since his time, the study of scholars versed in the languages of the same stock (including that of the Cuneiform Inscriptions) has done much to fix the meaning of the Zend, and to enable the learned to discriminate between dialectic varieties in the Zend books themselves. The use of the words Zend and Avesta is conventional, Avesta being supposed to mean "Scriptures," and Zend "oral tradition." The English reader has an opportunity of studying the whole of the Avesta in a work published at the cost of a Parsee gentleman—Spiegel's German translation of the Avesta rendered into English by Mr. Bleeck. Translations of parts of the Avesta may also be found in a volume of Essays by Haug. Unfortunately, the renderings of these two scholars exhibit considerable differences; but they agree sufficiently to shew that for general purposes the language is now fairly understood. I shall take the extracts which follow from Mr. Bleeck's translation, which seems to be done with care in a closely literal style.

There are no available data for fixing even approximately the age of Zoroaster or of the books of the Avesta. These books are almost without a history. The only existing MSS. of them are said to be comparatively modern. It is believed that their contents were not committed to writing till the time of the Sassanian dynasty (third century), having been handed down through long centuries by oral tradition. But there is sufficient proof from internal evidence of their great antiquity. A comparison of the Zend Avesta with the Vedas shews that the Zoroastrian religion and that of the earliest Vedas were branches of one stock; and there are allusions in the Avesta which point to an original home of the Aryan race in Bactria, from which one section of the race migrated to India, whilst the Iranian section moved westwards. It is conjectured that the separation of these two branches of the race was caused by a religious schism; and Mr. Ernest de Bunsen has seen in the story of Cain and Abel a mythical representation of this conflict. (See his book on The Hidden Wisdom, c. i.) The principal division of the Zend Avesta is into the Vendidad, the Yasna together with the Vispered, and the Khordah Avesta (or little Avesta). The Vendidad is the Zoroastrian Law-book. The Vispered and the Yasna form the liturgy for the priests. The Gâthâs, or hymns, in this part, are the most ancient compositions in the Avesta. The Khordah Avesta contains various prayers, intended for general use, and especially a series of Yashts, or invocations, addressed to the good Genii.

The special characteristic of this religion is the worship of Ahura-Mazda. True believers are called Mazdayasnians, (the word Yasna meaning sacrifice or worship,) and the law is called the good Mazdayasnian law. With Ahura-Mazda, but strictly subordinate to him, are associated a number of divinities, called Ameshaspentas, or Amshaspands. An evil power, named Angra-mainyus, (afterwards Ahrimanes,) works in opposition to Ahura-Mazda and the good creation, and he is aided by innumerable daevas, (devas, divs,) against which good Mazdayasmians are to wage war. The chief quality of Ahura-Mazda is purity, symbolized by light, and the counter-quality is pollution, symbolized by darkness. The ideas of light and darkness, purity and impurity, are perpetually recurring in the Avestan books; and the object of the worshipper is always to keep himself morally and ceremonially pure. Praise of all pure beings, and defiance of all impure, are the chief religious agencies for the elevation of the soul. Words, especially prayers and invocations, are the potent weapons for driving away evil. The great formative ideas of this religion are high and noble, and they are expressed with a striking simplicity. Indeed the reiteration of simple formulas conveys an impression of baldness and sterility: for good and for evil, speculation seems to have stopped short with the Zoroastrians at certain elementary conceptions with regard to the creation.

In the received accounts of the Zoroastrian religion, the most conspicuous feature of it is the Dualism represented by the names Ormuzd and Ahriman. These two powers are described as being co-eternal. But this does not appear to be stated in the Avesta. There Angro-mainyus, the Spirit of darkness, occupies much the same position as that occupied by the Devil in the Christian theology of most of the centuries of the Christian era. The good Creator and the good creation come first: afterwards the evil spirit seeks pertinaciously to spoil the good creation by introducing evil. But there is no vestige of any worship of the dark spirit: he is always to be overcome. There are two passages in the Gâthâs in which the two Powers, the good and the evil, are spoken of as more co-ordinate than they seem to be in the greater part of the Avesta (Yasna xxx. 3—6, and xliv. or xlv. 2), but in these very same hymns Ahura-Mazda is spoken of as primary and dominant.* Some

* Professor Rawlinson speaks of the older part of the Avesta as comparatively free from the Dualism which characterises the later part; and he refers to these passages in the Yasna as containing only the germ of the system subsequently developed. But I think there are no other passages in the Avesta so dualistic as these. (See Rawlinson's Ancient Monarchies, III. p. 105.)

allusions to the Infinite Time (zrvane akerane), or Eternity, appear to have been also systematized too rigidly into the conception of a Divine Abyss, answering to the En Soph of the Kabbalah, out of which Ahura-Mazda had birth. Ahura-Mazda is the Creator, and there seems to be no speculation as to his origin.

The first of the Yasnas, or liturgical invocations, begins thus :

1. "I invoke*: the Creator Ahura-Mazda, the Brilliant, Majestic, Greatest, Best, Most Beautiful,

2. The strongest, most intellectual, of the best body, the Highest through holiness;

3. Who is very wise, who rejoices afar,

4. Who created us, who formed us, who keeps us, the Holiest among the heavenly.

5. I invoke: Vohu-mano, Asha-vahista, Kshathra-vairya, Spenta-armaiti, Haurvat, and Ameretât."

These are the six Amesha-spentas, who have different provinces of creation under their care. I take the following account of them from Spiegel's note on this passage. 1. Vohu-mano (otherwise Bahman), the protector of all living creatures. [The name is said to mean Good Conscience, or Good Mind.] 2. Asha-vahista (Ardi-behist), the genius of fire. [The name = high piety, or best truth.] 3. Khshathra-vairya (Shahrevar) is the lord or protector of metals. The care of the poor is also entrusted to him. 4. Spenta-armaiti is a female genius, the goddess of the earth. In the older writings she is especially the goddess of wisdom; in the later, she bestows a good way of life, fluency of speech, &c. 5 and 6. Haurvat and Ameretât are almost always named together. The former is the lord of the waters, the latter of the trees.

In the later mythology, Ahura-Mazda is not reckoned

---

* I have substituted this simpler expression for "I invite and announce to" into which Bleeck has translated Spiegel's German rendering.

amongst the Amesha-spentas, and the number seven is completed by Sraosha or Serosh. His duty was to watch over the world, and especially to protect it in the night-time. The night is an especial development of the power of Angro-mainyus, and the Daevas work their deeds in darkness. Hence morning and evening prayers were offered to Sraosha. The cock also was sacred to him.

The following passage, relating to the Amesha-spentas, is from the Khordah-Avesta. "The strong Kingly Majesty praise we,

Which belongs to the Amesha-spentas, the shining, having efficacious eyes, great, helpful, strong, Ahurian, who are imperishable and pure.

Which are all seven of like mind, like speech, all seven doing alike, like is their mind, like their word, like is their action, like their Father and Ruler, namely, the Creator Ahura-Mazda.

* * * * * *

They it is who further the world at will so that it does not grow old and die, does not become corrupt and stinking, but ever-living, ever-profiting, a kingdom as one wishes it, that the dead may arise, and immortality for the living may come, which gives according to wish furtherance for the world.

The worlds which teach purity will be immortal, the Drukhs [the genius of Pollution] will disappear at the time. So soon as it comes to the pure to slay him and his hundred-fold seed, then is it (ripe) for dying and fleeing away." (Zamyad-Yasht, 14—20.)

Illustrations of the nature of Angro-mainyus, and of the power of *words*, or invocations, to overcome all evil spirits, may be found in the 19th Fargard, or Section, of the Vendidad.

" 1. From the north region, from the north regions,

rushed forth Angro-mainyus, he who is full of death, the Daeva of the Daevas.

2. Thus spake this evil-witting Angro-mainyus, who is full of death:

3. 'Drukhs! [Pollution,] run up, slay the pure Zarathustra.'

4. The Drukhs ran round him, the perishable, the deceiver of mortals.

5. Zarathustra recited the prayer Ahuna-vairya.* . . .

6. The Drukhs ran away from him grieved. . . .

7. The Drukhs answered him (Angro-mainyus): Tormentor, Angro-mainyus!

8. I do not see death in him, in the holy Zarathustra.

9. Full of brightness is the pure Zarathustra.

* * * * * *

16. Zarathustra informed Angro-mainyus: 'Evil-witting Angro-mainyus!

17. I will smite the creation which was created by the Daevas, I will smite the Nasus [genii of Pollution] which the Daevas have created,

18. I will smite thee . . ., until Saoshyans [more commonly Sosiosch] is born, the victorious, out of the water Kansaoya,

19. From the East region, from the Eastern regions.

[Sosiosch is the *Messiah* of the Zoroastrian traditions. The name means "He that will profit or help." Compare Jesus, Je-hoshua, *Help* of Jehovah. "It is the name," says Prof. Spiegel in his Commentary on the Vendidad, p. 421 (Leipsic, 1865,) "of the future Deliverer, who is to appear at the time of the Resurrection and establish the complete dominion of Ahura-Mazda on the Earth." As the

---

* A short formula of prayer, somewhat obscure, to be found at the beginning of the Khordah Avesta. The name appears under the form Honover, or Honwar. Great efficacy was ascribed to this *Word*. Manthra-spenta is the more general name for the Holy Word.

North is the quarter of the spirits of darkness, so whatever comes from Ahura-Mazda comes from the *East*.]

20. Him answered Angro-mainyus who has created the wicked creatures,

21. Do not slay my creatures, O pure Zarathustra!

22. Thou art the son of Pourashaspa, and hast life from a (mortal) mother!

23. Curse the good Mazdayasnian law, . . .

24. Him answered the holy Zarathustra:

25. I will not curse the good Mazdayasnian law;

26. Not if bones, soul, and vital power, were to separate themselves asunder.

27. Him answered Angro-mainyus who has created the evil creatures:

28. By whose word wilt thou smite, by whose word wilt thou annihilate, by what well-made arms (smite) my creatures, Angro-mainyus'?

29. Him answered the holy Zarathustra:

30. Mortar, cup, Haoma * [liturgical symbols, used in invocations,] and the words which Ahura-Mazda has spoken;

---

* The Hom, or Soma, juice, frequently mentioned in the Vedas. It is the juice of a plant called Asclepias acida, and in the Hindoo religion was drunk *fermented*. But there is no hint of *intoxication* by the drinking of the Hom juice in the Zoroastrian books; and it seems to me to be in accordance with the rest of this religion to regard this ceremony as a simple recognition of one of the benefits of creation, that, namely, conferred in the juice of wholesome plants. In a passage to be presently quoted, fire, water, cattle, trees, are enumerated together with the earth, the pure man, the stars, &c. as amongst the good things of Ahura's creation. All these are represented in the Zoroastrian worship. *Fire* is well known as a principal symbol of that worship. *Water* is represented by *holy water*, called Zaothra. Perhaps the Draonas, which were little round cakes, on which pieces of cooked flesh were placed, and which after certain prayers were eaten by the priests, may have had something to do with *earth*. In the praises and invocations, we read continually of the mythical Bull, or Cow, which represented cattle in general; and the use of cow's urine in purifications is (to this day) one of the chief features of the Mazdayasnian ritual. *Trees* are remembered in the consecration of the Baresma or Barsom, a bundle of twigs. Similarly, the consecration and drinking of the Hom may be an act of thanksgiving for the juices of all plants.

31. These are my best weapons;

32. By this word will I smite, by this word will I annihilate, by these well-formed weapons (smite), O evil Angromainyus;

33. Which Spenta-mainyus [the Good Spirit] created; he created in the infinite time;*

34. Which the Amesha-spentas created, the good Rulers, the wise."

The 11th Fargard gives rules as to the use of various prayers, especially the frequent repetition of the Ahunavairya, by which the evil spirit was to be driven away. The following passage enumerates the principal representatives of the pure creation. "I combat thee, O evil Angromainyus, (away) from the dwelling, from the fire, from the water, from the earth, from the cattle, from the trees, from the pure man, from the pure woman, from the stars, from the moon, from the sun, from the lights without beginning, from all the good things which Ahura has made which have a pure origin." (Vendidad, Fargard xi. 32.)

The name Daeva or Deva is that which in the Indo-Aryan family of languages signified a divine being. From the same root come Ζεύς and *deus*. But in the Zend Avesta, it always stands for an *evil* spirit. The Daevas are innumerable; they haunt darkness and corruption; their home is in the pit of darkness. They flock together in the places, called Dakhmas, where dead bodies are exposed:

"For that is the joy of the Daevas,
All to which stench cleaves.

For in these Dakhmas there are together dissolution, sickness, fever, uncleanness, cold fever, shivering, and old remains of hair." (Vendidad, Fargard vii. 143—145.)

---

* This is the zrvane-akerane, Time without bounds, mentioned above. It occurs again in this Fargard: "55. I praise the heaven, the self-created, the never-ending time, the air which works above."

Human beings who admit defilement are liable to be possessed by Drujas, (dæmons,) in this life, and will go to the abode of the Daevas in the next.

"They are not pure in life, and after death they take no share in Paradise.

They fill the place which is appointed for the wicked,
The dark, which comes from darkness,
Darkness.

This place ye make, ye are who are wicked, through your own deeds and your own law, the worst of places." (Fargard v. 173—177, vii. 54—57.)

Next to prayer, the cultivation of the ground was the best means of promoting purity.

"87. He who cultivates, this earth, O holy Zarathustra, with the left arm and the right, with the right arm and the left;

88. Then this earth speaks to him: Man, thou who cultivatest me with the left arm and the right, with the right arm and the left,

89. Always will I come hither and bear.

90. All food will I bear, together with the fruits of the field.

91. He who does not cultivate this earth, O holy Zarathustra, with the left arm and the right, with the right arm and the left,

92. Then this earth speaks to him: Man, thou who dost not cultivate me with the left arm and right, with the right arm and left,

93. Always thou standest there, going to the doors of others to beg for food:

94. Always they bring food to thee, thou who beggest lazily out of doors:

95. They bring to you out of their superfluity of good things.

96. Creator of the corporeal world, Pure One!

97. What is the increase of the Mazdayasnian law?

98. Then answered Ahura-Mazda: When one diligently cultivates corn, O holy Zarathustra.

99. He who cultivates the fruits of the field cultivates purity.

100. He promotes the Mazdayasnian law.

* * * * * *

105. When there are crops then the Daevas hiss,

106. When there are shoots then the Daevas cough,

107. When there are stalks then the Daevas weep,

108. When there are thick ears of corn then the Daevas fly.

109. There are the Daevas most smitten in the dwelling-places where the ears of corn are found.

110. To hell they go, melting like glowing ice.

111. After that let this Manthra [word] be recited:

112. No one, if he eats nothing, has any strength;

113. He is not able to be of pure conduct,

114. Not able to be employed in cultivation:

115. Since with food lives the whole corporeal world, and without food it dies." (Vendidad, Fargard iii.)

I will only add to these extracts a prayer, or rather *laud*, which is one of the favourite Mazdayasnian formulæ.

" 1. I praise the well-thought, well-spoken, well-performed, thoughts, words, and works.

2. I lay hold on all good thoughts, words, and works.

3. I abandon all evil thoughts, words, and works.

4. I bring to you, O Amesha-spentas,

5. Praise and adoration,

6. With thoughts, words, and works, with heavenly mind, the vital strength of my own body." (Yasna xii.)

We have no evidence that St. Paul ever came in contact with worshippers of Ahura-Mazda. But we know that there was a considerable population of Jews settled in

Babylonia, and spreading into Persia and Media, and that these for many generations had had opportunities of becoming acquainted with the Zoroastrian traditions: we know also that the systems of Gnosticism in the second and third centuries bore so strong a resemblance to the Persic mythology that it is impossible not to believe in some kind of connexion between them. The Epistle to the Colossians shews distinctly that speculations were prevalent amongst the Jews of Asia Minor, professing to be a higher $Γνῶσις$ or knowledge to be attained by the more learned and more religious, which remind us of the Gnostical and the Zoroastrian systems. Without, therefore, laying down any definite propositions as to the filiation of ideas which it is impossible to circumscribe within the limits of any one race or religion, we may imagine St. Paul to be confronted with the doctrines of Philo and of the Avesta, and we may conceive with certainty how he would deal with them. When he hears of various attempts to solve the mystery of creation; when he learns how men have travelled back from the definite to an Indefinite out of which the actual creation has grown; when he is told of a primal Fulness, of a development of the Divine nature in the process of creation, of a formative Word or words, of powers emanating from the supreme Divinity and ruling over different departments of the universe, of evil powers loving darkness and disorder which thwart the good purposes of the Creator and his instruments, of manifestations in which the good Creator reveals himself or some part of himself in order that he may drive out evil and establish the reign of harmony and happiness, of modes of approach to the heavenly powers by which men may rise above the general condition of sinful mortals;—St. Paul brings all such speculations to the test of his own theology, the theology of his Conversion. So far as they agree with the doctrine of the Father, the Son, and the Holy Spirit, he will gladly accept any expansion of view which they may suggest, he will use their phraseology. But they will not tempt him to give up his faith in Christ. He sees in Christ the true representation of the Eternal Fulness, the organ of creation, the head of all the powers which may be engaged in the evolution of nature, the prince of the kingdom of light, the one mediator between God and men, the one deliverer of the universe from all that troubles it. The way for men to come to God is to accept fellowship with Christ and to exercise the trust in God as a Father to which this fellowship with the Son entitles them. In being called to believe in Christ, they are called out of darkness into light, finding in him both peace with God and the true law of their life. They are bound to fight with Christ against all the powers of darkness; and in his triumph over these powers when he rose from the grave, they have the pledge of a final and complete victory.

THE END.

BY THE SAME AUTHOR.

ST. PAUL AND MODERN THOUGHT:

Remarks on some of the Views advanced in Professor Jowett's Commentary on St. Paul.

8vo. 2s. 6d.

SERMONS ON THE MANIFESTATION OF THE SON OF GOD.

With a Preface addressed to Laymen on the Present Position of the Clergy of the Church of England; and an Appendix on the Testimony of Scripture and the Church as to the possibility of Pardon in the Future State.

Fcap. 8vo. 6s. 6d.

THE WORK OF CHRIST;

OR,

THE WORLD RECONCILED TO GOD.

With a Preface on the Atonement Controversy.

Fcap. 8vo. 6s.

BAPTISM, CONFIRMATION, AND THE LORD'S SUPPER,
AS INTERPRETED BY THEIR OUTWARD SIGNS.

Three Expository Addresses for Parochial Use.

Limp cloth, 1s. 6d.

MACMILLAN AND CO. LONDON.

ECCE HOMO: A SURVEY OF THE LIFE AND WORK
OF JESUS CHRIST. Ninth Thousand. 8vo. cloth, price 10s. 6d.

THE HULSEAN LECTURES FOR 1865.

OUR LORD JESUS CHRIST THE SUBJECT OF GROWTH
IN WISDOM. Four Sermons (being Hulsean Lectures for 1865) preached before the University of Cambridge. To which are added, Three Sermons preached before the University of Cambridge in February, 1864. By the Rev. J. MOORHOUSE, M.A. St. John's College. Crown 8vo. cloth, price 5s.

DISCOURSES. By ALEXANDER J. SCOTT, M.A. Professor of Logic in Owen's College, Manchester. Crown 8vo. cloth, price 7s. 6d.

SERMONS. By the Rev. HENRY WOODWARD, M.A. formerly of Corpus Christi College, Oxford, Rector of Fethard, in the Diocese of Cashel. The Fifth Edition. Crown 8vo. cloth, price 10s. 6d.

THE HEAVENLY FATHER: LECTURES ON MODERN
ATHEISM. By ERNEST NAVILLE, Corresponding Member of the Institute of France, and formerly Professor of Philosophy in the University of Geneva. Translated by HENRY DOWNTON, M.A. English Chaplain at Geneva. Extra fcap. 8vo. price 7s. 6d.

NOTES OF THE CHRISTIAN LIFE. A Selection of Sermons by HENRY ROBERT REYNOLDS, B.A. President of Cheshunt College, and Fellow of University College, London. Crown 8vo. cloth, price 7s. 6d.

SERMONS PREACHED IN MANCHESTER. By ALEXANDER MACLAREN. New and Cheaper Edition. Fcap. 8vo. 4s. 6d.

VILLAGE SERMONS. By G. F. DE TEISSIER, B.D. Rector of Brampton, near Northampton, late Fellow and Tutor of Corpus Christi College, Oxford. Second Series, crown 8vo. cloth, 8s. 6d. Also First Series, crown 8vo. 9s.

MACMILLAN AND CO LONDON.

www.ingramcontent.com/pod-product-compliance
Lightning Source LLC
Chambersburg PA
CBHW030259170426
43202CB00009B/807